T0219964

IT Through Experiential Learning

Learn, Deploy and Adopt IT through Gamification

Shreekant W Shiralkar

Apress®

IT through Experiential Learning

Shreekant W Shiralkar
Mumbai, Maharashtra
India

ISBN-13 (pbk): 978-1-4842-2420-5   ISBN-13 (electronic): 978-1-4842-2421-2
DOI 10.1007/978-1-4842-2421-2

Library of Congress Control Number: 2016959190

Managing Director: Welmoed Spahr
Lead Editor: Celestin Suresh John
Technical Reviewer: Rakesh Mishra
Editorial Board: Steve Anglin, Pramila Balan, Laura Berendson, Aaron Black,
    Louise Corrigan, Jonathan Gennick, Robert Hutchinson, Celestin Suresh John,
    Nikhil Karkal, James Markham, Susan McDermott, Matthew Moodie, Natalie Pao,
    Gwenan Spearing
Coordinating Editor: Prachi Mehta
Copy Editor: Brendan Frost
Compositor: SPi Global
Indexer: SPi Global
Artist: SPi Global

Distributed to the book trade worldwide by Springer Science+Business Media New York, 233 Spring Street, 6th Floor, New York, NY 10013. Phone 1-800-SPRINGER, fax (201) 348-4505, e-mail orders-ny@springer-sbm.com, or visit www.springeronline.com. Apress Media, LLC is a California LLC and the sole member (owner) is Springer Science + Business Media Finance Inc (SSBM Finance Inc). SSBM Finance Inc is a **Delaware** corporation.

For information on translations, please e-mail rights@apress.com, or visit www.apress.com.

Apress and friends of ED books may be purchased in bulk for academic, corporate, or promotional use. eBook versions and licenses are also available for most titles. For more information, reference our Special Bulk Sales–eBook Licensing web page at www.apress.com/bulk-sales.

Any source code or other supplementary materials referenced by the author in this text are available to readers at www.apress.com. For detailed information about how to locate your book's source code, go to www.apress.com/source-code/. Readers can also access source code at SpringerLink in the Supplementary Material section for each chapter.

Printed on acid-free paper

Contents at a Glance

Contents

About the Author

Shreekant Shiralkar is a senior management professional with extensive experience in leading and managing business functions, as well as technology consulting. Shreekant played critical role in multiple transformation programs for Bharat Petroleum Corporation Ltd. including designing their supply chain strategy. He developed SAP Technology business for Tata Consultancy Services Ltd. by winning strategic clients in new and existing geographies, creating innovative service offerings, and playing a key role in organizational restructuring and formation of the Industry Solution Unit. Shreekant has established, developed, and diversified businesses, both within India and globally for Fortune 500 firms. He established the public service business in India for a global professional services company and provides consulting services in digital, technology, and operations. He launched and developed the Shell Gas business in India for a JV of Shell. Shreekant has authored bestseller books and white papers on technology and holds patents for innovations.

Acknowledgments

As I complete this book and reflect on its journey, my heart fills with gratitude for many individuals who helped me bring this book to you.

Foremost, I am indebted to Mr. Shrikant Gathoo, the Human Resources Director at Bharat Petroleum Corporation Ltd., who accepted an unusual idea of a virtual treasure hunt to facilitate technology adoption. His guidance and patronage enabled benefits from implementation of the idea and generated one of the earliest proof-points for me on the feasibility and application of experiential learning to an IT situation.

I thank Mr. Ranjit Menon, Sr. Managing Director at a global professional services company, for extending unstinted support and encouraging me to deploy my game-based approach to enable the adoption of new knowledge management platform and processes. I remain grateful for his patronage and confidence in me, which contributed to the success that helped me reinforce the value from the game-based approach premised on experiential learning.

I remain thankful to the executive leadership of S. H. Kelkar and Company, who were extremely encouraging to my game-based learning approach by enthusiastically participating in the activities. Their commitment to learn and acquire the most from the session made a permanent impression in my mind about them and also on the delivery of value from EL and the game-based approach.

I thank Mr. M. D. Agrawal, former CIO of India's second largest oil company and former president of the Computer Society of India, for his patronage in including me as faculty for Process and Change Management in his management development program for CIOs of leading companies in India and for helping me showcase the delivery of value from the game-based approach.

Translating complicated ideas and concepts into easily understood text needs facilitation. I express my gratitude to Mr. Sharad Awasthi, my colleague and author, who supported me in my journey from the beginning and helped me shape my ideas into the book.

To refine and communicate my experiments and ideas through the book needed much more than friendly encouragement and suggestions, and I feel privileged and indebted to have friends like Krishnan Subramaniam and Atul Mathur, who patiently read my gibberish thoughts and provided valuable suggestions that contributed to manifesting this book from an idea.

I thank my friends Shirish Dandekar and Srinivas Kale and my colleagues Nadeem Akhtar and Deepak Purnaye, Deepak Sawant, Onkar Sapre, and Jayant Daithankar, who spared time to read rough script and made valuable suggestions.

I thank Mr. Jayant Akut, Executive Director [Information Services] IS Group Refineries at Bharat Petroleum, for sparing his time to read the raw script and sharing his feedback, which added to my confidence. I would like to express my sincere gratitude to the Apress team, namely, Celestin Suresh, Jim Marakham, and Prachi Mehta, as well as the Technical Reviewer Mr. Rajesh Mishra, who partnered this journey of shaping the script of the book; in particular, Jim worked on some of the script too and helped me refine the articulation.

Finally, I wish to express my gratitude to two most important people, who are the reason for my every endeavor, my lovely children, Shashank and Rohan. Here's a part of my poem dedicated to them:

Holding you first time, moment and meaning of life defined...

A smile on your face, introduced the divined...

Movement of a man into father,

Eager to wing your dreams farther,

Ever-changing this journey of life manifold...

You were, are and always be my world.

Preface

In my career journey of over 29 years, I witnessed metamorphosis of the back-office EDP (electronic data processing) unit into a core strategic function, now termed the Information Technology (IT) function. During this journey, I moved from business functions to the IT function, contributed to many large-scale IT and organization transformation programs, and recognized the power of experiential learning on their success.

In early 2015, I was invited as guest faculty to deliver a lecture on "Project Management" to a class of engineering students. For groundwork, I gathered information about the course curriculum and the relevance of guest lecture from a project management practitioner. I chose to focus on key factors for successfully managing projects and engaging students through a game, instead of delivering lectures and talking about the terms and concepts. The session received huge appreciation from students and faculty for its effectiveness in facilitating learning. A colleague who witnessed the session remarked that many important aspects like project management are best learned by experience during actual work rather than curriculum and books. This remark sparked the idea and motivation to fill the void by bringing awareness about experiential learning and its application through games and provide resources for academia and professionals to apply, adopt, and deliver IT.

As time went by, the idea of the book started taking shape from mere thoughts into scribbles, leading eventually to shaping the table of content and chapters. The process picked up momentum as the publishing commenced and the focus shifted to articulation and presentation of the idea into a form that readers will comprehend and apply.

The core theme of the book revolves around application of experiential learning through games. The book shows readers how experiential learning can be used to overcome the challenges posed in applying, adopting, and delivering IT to their business needs through innovative, game-based approach with detailed explanations and suggestions. The content is crafted to be easy to understand and aided by illustrations and sample artifacts. The book also provides guidance to expand, experiment with, and bring variations to applying the approach. It is my hope that the book will become an indispensable resource for academia and management professionals engaged in IT.

I am excited to publish this book, and I hope you will enjoy reading it and experience the effectiveness of experiential learning by applying the approach detailed in the book. May this book become one of your most valued resources.

CHAPTER 1

Introduction

Business environments are rapidly changing, and information technology (IT) is at
the core of such a change. Innovations in technology, along with completely new
business models, are part of the rapid change that is forcing corporate and management
professionals to learn, deploy, and adopt IT for survival and competitive advantage. IT is
no longer just a back-office function, but a strategic business function as well.

The success of IT hinges largely on the ability of all the stakeholders to understand,
apply, and adopt it. There are numerous examples of large IT investments proving to
be wasted, due to lack of understanding, incorrect application, or faltering during its
adoption.

My objective in this book is to raise awareness about how experiential learning (EL)
can help overcome challenges posed in learning, applying, adopting, and delivering
IT. EL is at the core of the game-based approach across scenarios in IT; for example, a
treasure hunt for learning about new technology, and a team game to appreciate the
implications of IT. The approach will enable gaining speed in learning IT as well as longer
retention span of the key concepts. This book's game-based approach to learning IT is
intended to ensure that IT delivers on its promises and provides a compelling advantage
over conventional methods like lectures and reading.

This chapter will introduce you to the fundamental concepts and relevance of EL
along with an overview of game-based approach scenarios in IT, which are detailed in the
subsequent chapters.

Let me briefly describe EL and key concepts.

Experiential Learning

EL is defined as the process of learning by experience. EL is far more effective than
conventional processes and learning methods like lectures or reading. EL's method
focuses on creating experiences that facilitate learning which is self-governed, that is
to say without any explicit external intervention, which would otherwise control and
guide the knowledge acquisition process. The speed at which learning happens in EL is
much higher than any conventional process of learning, and by channeling the learning
through games, engagement with the subject is higher, which results in a higher degree of
knowledge retention as well.

© Shreekant W Shiralkar 2016
S. W. Shiralkar, *IT Through Experiential Learning*, DOI 10.1007/978-1-4842-2421-2_1

To understand and appreciate the fundamental concepts on EL, Edgar Dale's Cone of Experience is reproduced in Figure 1-1. Edgar Dale was an American educationist known for his work on effectiveness in education and more specifically the Cone of Experience. The Cone of Experience relates to how the ability to learn and apply information is affected by the way information is encountered or experienced.

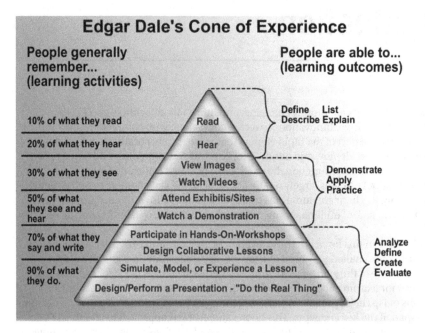

Figure 1-1. *Edgar Dale's Cone of Experience*

[https://commons.wikimedia.org/wiki/File:Edgar_Dale%27s_cone_of_learning.png]

You will note that according to Edgar Dale's Cone of Experience, the ability to analyze, define, create, and evaluate is acquired only after participation and self-experience; and in contrast, conventional methods of training or learning such as reading, hearing, and so on do not develop the ability to apply learning and produce results.

The average retention rates associated with EL are high, in the 80%–90% area. These statistics are proven by third-party research shown in this learning pyramid: a well-known piece of research from the National Training Laboratory in Bethel, Maine (Figure 1-2).

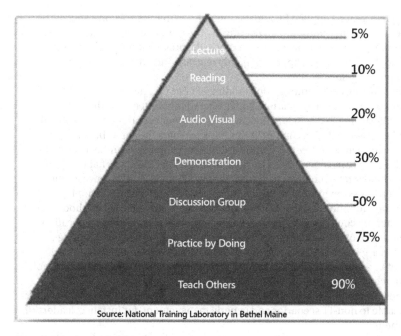

Lecture	5%
Reading	10%
Audio Visual	20%
Demonstration	30%
Discussion Group	50%
Practice by Doing	75%
Teach Others	90%

Source: National Training Laboratory in Bethel Maine

Figure 1-2. *Retention levels*

You will note that conventional learning methods of listening and reading (typically lecture and reading based) fall into the 5%–10% retention category.

Further, the success of EL has been also discussed by educational theorist David Kolb in his groundbreaking book *Experiential Learning: Experience as the Source of Learning and Development* (Prentice-Hall, 1984). The book highlighted that adults learn best through discovery and experience.

To reap the benefits of EL, such as the ability to analyze and produce results, as well as ensuring a high degree of retention of knowledge, I developed a game-based approach of learning through discovery and experience in a joyful environment.

Experiential Learning in the IT World

This book evolved from a leadership development program I attended many decades back. The program had team-based games, and each game was designed to create an experience for learning, rather than regular teaching methods like classroom lectures. I noted that the games in the program had applied EL to facilitate understanding the subject of leadership. Until then, for years, I had read most of the prescribed books on the subject, attended sessions on leadership by globally recognized faculties, and worked for very successful leaders, and yet had not gained as much understanding on leadership as I did while playing games in that program. I was also startled by the speed at which I learned key aspects of leadership with a very high degree of comprehension. Best of all, I observed that I did not have to put much effort into recalling the lessons. The program consolidated my conviction about the effectiveness of EL and its application though a game-based approach to situations like learning leadership.

In subsequent years, I applied EL and its principles to many situations, specifically for learning, deploying, adopting, and delivering IT. The outcomes were much more successful than those produced by regular methods like presentation, lectures, and reading. I found the game-based approach highly relevant and effective for learning, teaching, and problem-solving scenarios.

I consider learning and gaining understanding of IT as comparable to learning cycling or swimming; they can be learned and mastered most effectively through experience. And learning in a light and fun-filled environment creates a high probability of interest and engagement. The content in this book explains the game-based approach for creating an experience that fosters learning, deploying, adopting, and delivering IT.

Knowledge society in general and IT professionals in specific have challenges in keeping pace with the rapid changes caused by innovation in IT and its downstream impact on the business environment. Stakeholders need to understand technology, its application and adoption, at a pace that is far more than conventional methods like reading and listening could enable. A game-based approach premised on application of EL is therefore one of the best alternatives for learning, deploying, and adopting IT. The game-based approach contained in this book can therefore benefit leaders and practitioners of IT as well as corporate trainers and educators. This approach will enable maximizing outcomes from your investment in IT.

In the book, the game-based approach is applied for IT scenarios; they are, however, equally applicable to non-IT scenarios and generic management, for instance, leadership skill development.

Each scenario of application of the approach is detailed with explanations aided by visual illustration and step-by-step processes, along with examples, for real-world application that should be both immediate and beneficial.

What to Expect . . .

Each chapter in this book presents the fun, adventure, and challenge of various games. Each scenario features a narrative, goal, flow, consolidation, and feedback process. The final chapter will introduce possibilities for modification of the games explained in the chapters, and invite you to innovate by creating new games and applying the approach to newer situations. The following are the scenarios covered in this book:

- Chapter 2: Aircraft Manufacturing Game. A competitive team game of making and selling airplanes to create experience for learning the impact of system integration and information on the profitability of the enterprise.

- Chapter 3: Bidding Game. A game for multiple teams competing and bidding for points based, on knowledge/expertise within the team to generate rapid learning on a new and abstract subject.

- Chapter 4: Blindfold Game. A competitive game for performing a task blindfolded under the plan and guidance of a leader, to mentor new leaders and establish a framework for successful teamwork.

- Chapter 5: Arrangement Game. An exercise to help participants experience the challenge of competing constraints and its impact on the collective outcome. Each player is tagged with a number, and there's a collective arrangement that needs to be accomplished within a time constraint.

- Chapter 6: Treasure Hunt. A virtual treasure hunt designed to accelerate the adoption of new technology and/or process change.

- Chapter 7: R2R Workshop. A game on communication and its impact on a globally spread team delivering an IT solution.

After introducing you to the basics of EL and its relevance, each of the chapters is dedicated to explaining application of EL to a specific situation in IT. The context for each application is covered in brief with details on design and execution tasks for the game or activity. Efforts are put into detailing the design and execution tasks in the easiest language, and the tasks are complemented by illustrations or visuals on the basis of actual situations.

In the concluding chapter, I have provided few more scenarios and motivation and guidance for application of the game-based approach to different situations in IT by creating new games.

Summary

In the era of the knowledge economy, higher effectiveness in learning is far more justified than ever before. Dynamic and rapid evolution in the ecosystem has reduced the time available to learn. The situation is compounded by the need for retention of knowledge with deeper comprehension of the subject. Applying EL is therefore a necessity in today's environment, especially to IT situations.

Now that you are aware of the EL and its relevance in the IT context, and also of how learning is most effective when facilitated through a game-based approach. The following chapters will explain details on applying EL for learning, deploying, adopting, and delivering IT through the game-based approach.

CHAPTER 2

■ ■■ ■

Aircraft Manufacturing Game

Context: Understanding Impact and Benefits of ERP

Lack of knowledge and awareness about any concept creates a mystery around it. Generating interest and engagement provides opportunities to break the barriers that are holding back awareness and knowledge. Creating experience around the concept and its application enables unraveling the complexities, raising awareness of its finer aspects and thereby developing a deeper comprehension, thus facilitating movement from mystery to mastery.

Most business colleges and universities use, case studies as a teaching supplement, to enable students to learn advanced concepts like ERP (enterprise resource planning) and its necessary place in an enterprise. Case studies or similar approaches for learning supplements, however, lack effectiveness. Applying experiential learning via gamification facilitates experiencing the complexities of the concept, helping participants to comprehend the concept far more deeply. Students are invited to participate and play different roles in the game. Engaging students in a game, enable them to experience near-real-world situations, including making choices and taking decisions, instead of imagining the situations and hypothesizing the concept and its complexities. Learning gained from such a direct and personal encounter with the concept is therefore far more effective.

I had undertaken an assignment to start a course on ERP for a postgraduate management institute. Most of the students did not have any exposure to working of an enterprise, and thus any expectations, for them to appreciate the importance of ERP for an enterprise were misplaced. I further realized that explaining ERP using conventional methods—lecture, audiovisuals, and case study—would be too slow, even disregarding their intrinsic limitations, such as audience misinterpretations of oral or visual explanations. I therefore designed a game that involved students in a simulated enterprise environment so that they could experience the situation both, with and without an ERP solution. The level of knowledge gained by students was later evaluated by a panel consisting of the CIO of an ERP user company and a senior IT professional. The panel members were thoroughly impressed by the depth of comprehension of the subject demonstrated by students, as it was much higher than that of similar students from other institutes, with whom they had met for similar assessments. They were most impressed to find that students had acquired deeper understanding of ERP in an extremely short period.

© Shreekant W Shiralkar 2016
S. W. Shiralkar, *IT Through Experiential Learning*, DOI 10.1007/978-1-4842-2421-2_2

This is the premise of the game that will be explained in this chapter. The game introduces a fun element in experiencing how an ERP solution enables the enterprise to generate efficiency and effectiveness, thereby facilitating an accelerated comprehension of the concept.

The Aircraft Manufacturing Game is played by students in teams. Teams compete to generate the highest profit within the same set of situations and constraints. The game is designed to represent a real-world business environment in the most simplistic form possible and to facilitate experiencing the subtler aspects of ERP, including how it helps to generate efficiency and makes higher profitability more probable.

The competitive aspect triggers intensity and depth of the experience. Game elements aid in generating higher interest levels without stress (Figure 2-1). Real-world simulation facilitates comprehension of the subject—for instance, how ERP generates instant visibility of the impact of each transaction on profitability.

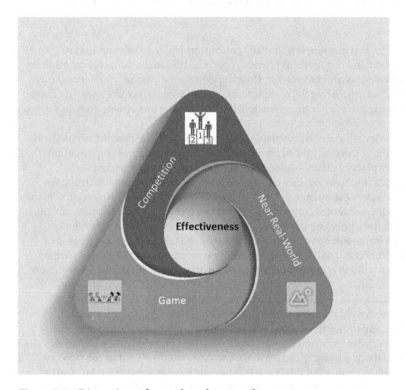

Figure 2-1. *Dimensions of game-based approach*

Here's an overview of the game:

1. Buy paper (the paper represents raw material).

2. Convert the paper into paper aircraft (this represents the manufacturing process).

3. Sell these paper aircraft to customer.

The process to create a paper aircraft is shown in Figure 2-2.

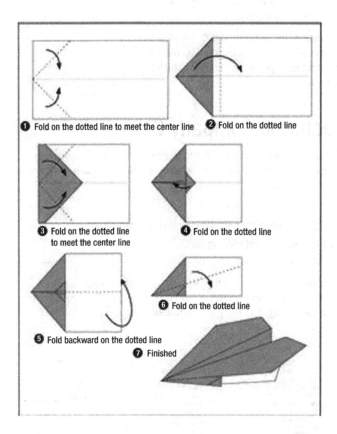

Figure 2-2. *How to create an aircraft from paper*

Each team consists of five players, with one team member taking the lead and others performing specific roles as follows:

1. The leader represents the CEO of the company and is responsible for generating profits. The leader plans strategy; makes decisions about bank credit, raw material (i.e., paper) inventory, discounts for preferred buyers, and so on; and in general, instructs other team members.

2. Procurement is responsible for sourcing raw material (i.e., paper) as per guidance of the leader and passing it over to the Production team member.

3. Production is responsible for creating aircraft from paper and handing them over to the Sales team member.

4. Sales is responsible for selling aircraft to customer, primarily by engaging in negotiation and closing the deal by taking money and giving aircraft to buyer.

5. Finance is responsible for continuously recording money transactions with the bank, the paper seller, and the aircraft buyer for and calculating profit and keeping the leader informed about numbers.

Aircraft Manufacturing Company Game

Considering the complexity of the game, it is essential to demonstrate a typical business cycle before actual play. The demo cycle will help participants to play the game well and, more importantly, experience learning.

■ **Note**   Cycle = Complete set of multiple transactions within a quarter involving converting paper into aircraft and selling and earning profit.

Let us now examine the task-level details of the Aircraft Manufacturing Game, beginning with preparation and prerequisite material and continuing with its execution, including steps to consolidate learning after the game is finished. An overview of the entire activity is shown in Figure 2-3.

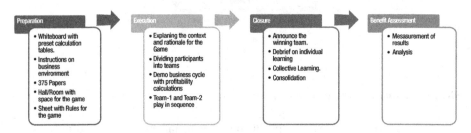

Figure 2-3. *Aircraft Manufacturing Game process flow*

Complete details of the activities in the process flow are described in detail in the following sections.

Activity

The following is a description of the business environment. The aircraft manufacturing company has one plant. It sources raw material from a single vendor and sells its product to a single airline. Manufacturing infrastructure and labor are limited. The company borrows funds from a single bank at a simple interest rate. Team plays as the company and generates profit by increasing the price or reducing the cost within one business cycle while announcing the quarterly balance sheet to stakeholders at the close of each quarter.

Players on both teams are instructed that they are start-ups and that they need to plan their strategy accordingly. Also, both teams will operate within identical business situations:

- Bank interest rates in the initial business cycle and successive cycles are as follows:

    - Cycle 1: 3% up to 100,000 Mil USD and 2% for any amount above 100,000 Mil USD.

    - Cycles 2 & 3: 4% up to 100,000 Mil USD and 3% for any amount above 100,000 Mil USD.

    - Cycle 4: 3.5% up to 100,000 Mil USD and 2.5% for any amount above 100,000 Mil USD.

    - Cycle 5: 2.5% up to 100,000 Mil USD and 2% for any amount above 100,000 Mil USD.

- Raw material vendor with the same price for paper supply per business cycle as follows:

    - Cycle 1: $10,000 per paper for the first 10 papers, $5,000 per paper for 10 to 20 papers, and $3,000 for 21 or more papers.

    - Cycle 2: $15,000 per paper for the first 10 papers, $10,000 per paper for 10 to 20 papers, and $7,000 for 21 or more papers.

    - Cycles 3 & 4: $20,000 per paper for first 10 papers, $15,000 per paper for 10 to 20 papers, and $10,000 for 21 or more papers.

    - Cycle 5: $9,000 per paper for first 10 papers, $7,000 per paper for 10 to 20 papers, and $5,000 for 21 or more papers.

- Manpower costs will remain same for all business cycle with $500 per business cycle per person.

- Manufacturing capability per person will remain constant: aircraft making will be fixed to 15 aircraft per minute (i.e., the maximum number of aircraft that can be manufactured per business cycle will be 75, and thus teams will be limited to 375 total for the five cycles).

- The notional price of one aircraft is around $35,000; however, this can be changed through negotiation with buyer.

- The maximum number of aircraft that the purchaser or airline can buy is 75.

- The only difference between the two teams is that one team will get a whiteboard to use for continuous update of transactions and calculation of profitability posts each transaction, as shown in Figure 2-4.

11

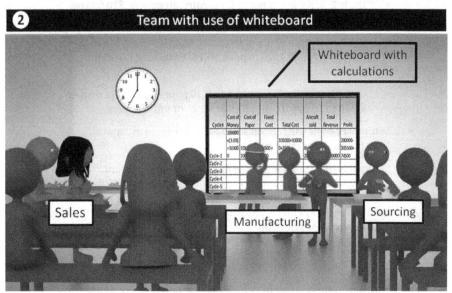

Figure 2-4. *Two teams playing Aircraft Manufacturing Game*

A sample calculation for demonstrating how the profit would be calculated is illustrated in Figure 2-5.

Cycle#	Cost of Money	Cost of Paper	Fixed Cost (Manpower)	Total Cost	Aircraft sold	Total Revenue	Profit
Cycle-1	100000 x(1.03) =10300 0	10X10000= 100000	5x500 = 2500	103000+10000 0+2500 = 205500	8x35000= 280000	280000	280000- 205500= 74500
Cycle-2							
Cycle-3							
Cycle-4							
Cycle-5							

Figure 2-5. *Sample calculation sheet*

After the teams are given the aforesaid business environment variables, it is explained to them that certain elements can be decided and changed by them as per their strategy:

- Amount of money to be borrowed from time to time.

- Number of team members.

- Raw material (i.e., number of papers to be procured, procurement frequency).

- Discounts or rebates to be given to airline/buyer for incentivizing aircraft sold.

Required Materials

- Instruction and regulations sheet for each role holder in two sets for each game play.

- Stack of 375 papers for each game play.

- Individual worksheet for money borrowed/interest liability, money owed to supplier, money owed to people for work, money paid for raw material/finished product inventory, money earned through sale of aircraft after netting of the discount/rebates paid to the airline/buyer.

- Whiteboard with the calculation sheet (refer Figure 2-5) in tabular form for continual calculation of profitability from transactions of purchase and sale.

- Set of FAQ to respond to questions.

- Means to record the activity over a video for replay during debrief.

- Stopwatch for measuring and monitoring time and maintaining participation statistics.

- Prizes and rewards that help promote the competition in form of a winner's trophy, gifts, and tokens of appreciation across many categories. Recognizing every participant will support higher participation and ensure accomplishment of the intended objectives. While recognition by itself could be attractive enough, other prizes or rewards, limited in number to maintain a spirit of competition, should be even more attractive.

Once all the preparation is complete, execution of the game can begin.

Execution

All the participants are explained the context and rationale for the game: that is, how an enterprise engaged in sourcing material and adding value by transforming it, sells this value-added product at a profit.

A business cycle with profitability calculations is demonstrated to all the participants so as to establish the process of the game and initiate participants into the game.

You must ensure that the demonstration is detailed, including an explanation of the context of each of the activities and their relevance to the process of an enterprise as well as the impact on the outcome of the game.

Ten volunteers are invited to play the game, and then they form teams and identify leaders for the two teams.

Each of the teams has to complete the activity about 30 minutes. This includes the 2 minutes given for calculations at 5-minute intervals; in other words, processing of the balance sheet at each quarter is to be done within the time constraint. Teams perform five consecutive business cycles, with each cycle consisting of 5 minutes. At the end of each business cycle they get time for 2 minutes to calculate the profit made, which is added to their team score. After completion of the five cycles, the winner is announced on the basis of the cumulative score for the five cycles. The team objective is to make a higher profit than the competing team.

On the basis of the profits, the winner of the game is announced and participants are engaged in debrief through capturing their experience and learning on the whiteboard.

Once the game is over, observations from experience are collected and crystallized in learning in the debrief section.

Debrief

The learning gained through the experience, while playing the game, needs to be articulated and consolidated. Debrief is a process that aids in articulating the learning that students gained during the game that simulated the enterprise environment. Each student who played the game or watched the two teams play the game has experienced the situation and will be able to articulate learning about the differences between the teams' performance and efficiency with and without the whiteboard that relates to an ERP solution.

The debrief process begins with asking the leader of the first team to share experience, especially after observing the advantage the second team had of regular updates and the direct visibility of the effect of each transaction on profitability by use of the whiteboard.

Subsequently, the leader of the second team shares learning about how their team was enabled by the whiteboard to generate profit, and how it could have been leveraged further to raise the score even higher.

The process is followed with asking each of the first team's members, along with his or her counterpart on the second team, about their experiences, and the differences between the two are noted on a well-displayed whiteboard.

Students who were not part of either team will also have new observations and learnings, and these are similarly captured.

Key points are noted on a whiteboard after discussion and consensus, with the observer or student sharing the learning. The process of writing on the whiteboard also allows time for each student to reflect the uniqueness of his or her observations and share with the rest of the students, and also triggers others to reflect and share their learning (Figure 2-6). The process also reinforces the learning.

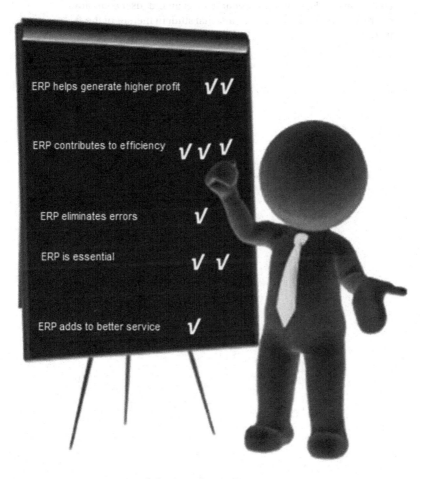

Figure 2-6. *Instructor consolidating collective learning*

After consolidation of the learning, it's recommended to conduct a benefit assessment exercise, to track and monitor the gains from application of the gamification.

Benefit Assessment

The level of knowledge gained by participant can be evaluated through the following:

- Written test, possibly with multiple-choice questions. The questions could begin with basic aspects and conclude with advanced aspects.

- A competition on the subject with students from other institutes.

- An assessment by an external panel from industry. The panel could consist of a senior professional from an ERP user company, a senior IT professional, and an internal student mentor of the institute.

CHAPTER 3

■ ■ ■

Bidding Game

Context: Collaborative Learning and Collective Understanding of ERP

During our school days, my friends and I frequently engaged in discussing specific topics from our textbooks. Each one of us comprehended a specific aspect of the larger subject, and when we shared understanding or knowledge of the topic, we found that our collective understanding helped us raise each individual's understanding much faster and deeper than individually struggling to comprehend the subject. Later, we even formalized the process during the examination period as we found the process helping learn quickly. During my college days, we practiced the technique further by forming study groups, and when having difficulty understanding a topic, we broke it into subtopics and distributed among the group for learning parts individually and then collectively sharing it with the rest of the group. The process helped each one of us in comprehending knowledge which appeared difficult and complex to us as individuals. The results of learning through a process of discussion were impressive and gave me insight into a few aspects of the concept formally known as "cooperative learning," which defines the process of learning together rather than being passive individual receivers of knowledge (e.g., teacher lecturing and students hearing). This process allows learners to use cognitive skills of questioning and clarifying, extrapolating and summarizing.

In one of my assignments, I was engaged to train the top management of an organization on ERP and the impact of its implementation. I anticipated that it would be a huge challenge to engage top executives in this training, as most would have had some understanding already, and applying a conventional training process risked losing their attention if my co-trainer or I fell short of their expectations. While individually each top executive may have had generic knowledge of ERP, they certainly lacked comprehensive knowledge, and more specifically a seamless collective understanding of the subject, without any gaps due to individual interpretations or exposures. The task, therefore, was multifaceted: on one hand, I had to get them interested in learning aspects of which they lacked knowledge, and on the other, I had to encourage them to share their individual understandings of the subject, facilitating development of a collective learning.

© Shreekant W Shiralkar 2016

S. W. Shiralkar, *IT Through Experiential Learning*, DOI 10.1007/978-1-4842-2421-2_3

For a top executive, it is expected that he or she needs to take calculated risks in almost every key decision, whether it's bidding for a large contract or establishing price point while taking a privately held organization for public trading. The process of bidding involves awareness of collective knowledge of capability, assessment about competition, and expertise to apply judgment based on rational (and some irrational) criteria. In the knowledge-driven economy, the contributions of each employee, regardless of level, add up to the collective capability of the organization.

With a view to facilitate collective learning in the shortest possible time for these top executives, I conceived a "Bidding Game" that leveraged cooperative learning to teach the ERP solution and the impact of its implementation in one session. The result in of Bidding Game was outstanding.

This is the premise of the game that will be explained in this chapter. The game also helps induce elements of social skills like effective communication and interpersonal and group skills in learning an otherwise abstract and complex subject.

The Bidding Game is a game played by all the participants divided into two or more teams. Teams compete on the strength of their collective knowledge of the subject. The game concludes after the collective learning on a specific subject is acquired to the appropriate level on all the essential aspects. The game format provides encouragement to each participant to contribute his or her knowledge of the subject and helps the team to win. A notional value attached to the correct and complete response helps measure the level of knowledge among participants. The competition is premised on the accuracy of the initial bid, which adds a flavor of bidding.

Figure 3-1 will help you visualize the setting created for the participants of the Bidding Game.

Figure 3-1. *Instructor inviting bids*

In a hall, participants will be seated in a U-shaped arrangement, facing the projector screen. The hall will have two whiteboards on either side of the projector screen. One of the whiteboards will be titled "Knowledge Bid" and will display the bids by participating teams.

The second whiteboard will record the actual earnings or the SCORE for each of the teams. The projector screen will be used to publish the question for each of the bid, and the instructor will allow the teams to respond in sequence and will record the score on the whiteboard on the basis of the accuracy and completeness of response by the team (Figure 3-2).

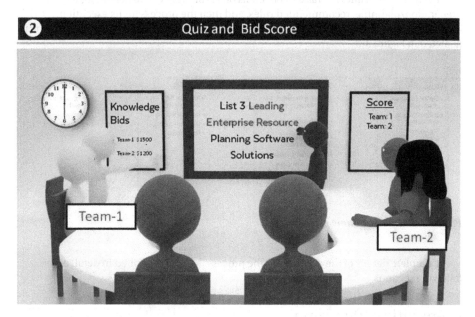

Figure 3-2. *Instructor inviting response to question*

In designing the Bidding Game, the elements of competition and encouraging discussion on each aspect form the core theme. The competitive aspect triggers speed, the game element induces interest without force or pressure, and finally discussions and sharing of knowledge facilitate desired coverage of the subject—for instance, technical nuances and features offered by new technology and/or processes, channelling an accelerated Learning and Collective Understanding new technology and/or processes.

Bidding Game Design

To design the Bidding Game, I recommend ensuring that the pace of learning is accelerated gradually, and that learning begins with basic aspects and moves on to the advanced and complex aspects in sequence instead of beginning with complex subjects and then concluding with basics. In the design of the sequence, care has to be exercised in segregating the basic and must-learn aspects from the "nice-to-know" aspects, and design should ensure accomplishing learning of basic and must-learn ones while provisioning for nice-to-know types based on the interest and appetite of the participants. Design the sequence in such a way that initially the participant need to spend less time and are encouraged toward the game and competition, while later parts of the sequence should ensure that participants spend more time in discussions and staying ahead of competition.

The objective—rapid development of collective learning of technology and/or new processes—necessitates a short duration of the Bidding Game.

Let us now examine the task-level details of the Bidding Game beginning with preparation/planning, recommended rules, and then the process for its execution, including steps to consolidate learning after conclusion. An overview of the entire game is depicted in Figure 3-3.

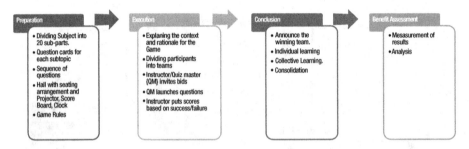

Figure 3-3. *Bidding Game process flow*

Complete details of the activities in the process flow are described in detail in the following sections.

Preparation/Planning

- Divide the subject into 20 subtopics that cover the subject comprehensively.

- Create a question for each of the subtopics.

- Create a sequence of questions in a way that gradually raises the level of knowledge.

- Segment the questions into three levels: Rookie, Advanced, and Expert.

- Assign different values to questions from the three sets, for example, $100 per question from the Rookie level, $200 per question from the Advanced level, and $300 per question from the Expert level.

- Develop a clear rule set for the Bidding Game that can be used to explain the game to the participants.

- Have a scoreboard that displays the bid value of the team and also their score during the progress of the game (use the whiteboard marker pens).

- Have a large clock for monitoring time and identify assistants for keeping time and recording the score.

Recommended Rules

- The winner is chosen on the basis of two parameters: high score as well as that which is closest to its bid.

- Each wrong or incomplete response has a loss of value (i.e., negative marking); for example, a $50 penalty for each wrong or incomplete response.

- $50 is deducted from the value of a passed-over question or a partly answered question.

- The completeness of the response to a question can be challenged by competing teams to apply penalty and reduce the score.

- There's a limit of 5 minutes for responding to each question. Each round could begin sequence in a way that provides a fair chance to all the teams.

Once all the preparation is completed, the game can begin.

Execution

1. All the participants are told the context and rationale for the game (i.e., what ERP is and the importance of each of them having a collective understanding of the subject, which would maximize benefit from its implementation). Also, it should be explained how playing a game such as this can increase individual understanding much faster and more deeply than individually struggling to comprehend the subject in isolation.

2. Participants are divided into teams. Team formation can be done in any way that generates nearly equal numbers of participants for each team (dividing the room, counting off by twos, etc.)

3. The instructor/quiz master (QM) invites bids from each of the teams, which are recorded on the whiteboard for everyone to see.

4. The instructor launches the first question on the screen and invites the first team to take its chance, while the timekeeper monitors the time taken by the responding team.

5. On the basis of correctness and completeness of the response, the instructor assigns a score to the team, which is recorded on the second whiteboard.

6. In case the question is passed to the second team and they are able to respond correctly and completely, the reduced score is recorded.

7. In case the question is not answered or is incompletely responded by any of the teams, the instructor shares the correct and complete answer and the subject is discussed and clarified.

8. The process continues until the subject is completely covered.

9. The instructor tallies the scores for the teams and announces the winner on the basis of the high score and the bid accuracy.

Once the game is over, observations from experience are collected and crystallized in learning in the next section.

Conclusion

- The learning gained through the game needs to be articulated and consolidated. Debrief is a process that will aid in articulating learning that participants gained during the game.

- The process of debrief begins with each participant sharing learning, specifically something that has changed their understanding about the subject during the game.

- Each participant would have learned something new, be it a very basic addition to earlier knowledge of the subject or very complex information that the participant hadn't ever known before.

- The individual learnings are recorded on a whiteboard, which helps in crystallizing and consolidating collective understanding on the subject.

- Once the game is over, the learning can be consolidated by presenting additional material by way of slides, videos, and so on.

Sample Artifacts

With a view to facilitate the immediate application of the approach in the chapter, a sample list of questions on ERP and Big Data along with an illustrative score sheet with result, are provided in the following section. The correct responses from multiple choices, are identified in bold.

Sample Question Cards: ERP

1. What is the extended form of ERP?

    a. Enterprise Retail Process

    b. **Enterprise Resource Planning**

    c. Earning Revenue and Profit

    d. None of the above

2. Real time in the context of ERP relates to which of the following?

    a. Time shown in the computer system synchs with your watch

    b. **Processes/events happen per transaction at the same instant**

    c. Both of the above

    d. None of the above

3. What does "SOA" stand for in relation to ERP system architecture?

    a. **Service-Oriented Architecture**

    b. System of Accounts

    c. Statement of Account

    d. None of the above

4. Which of these is not a packaged ERP?

    a. SAP

    b. Oracle

    c. **Windows**

    d. JD Edwards

5. In the context of packaged ERP, do "Customization" and "Configuration" refer to the same process, or are they different?

    a. Same

    b. **Different**

    c. Don't know

6. Materials Management in ERP helps to/esnure ?

   a. Increase of inventory

   b. **Inventory is well balanced**

   c. Both of the above

   d. None of the above

7. Sales and Distribution Module in ERP helps in which of the following?

   a. **Increased customer service**

   b. Reduced customer service

   c. Both of the above

   d. None of the above

8. Financial and Controlling Module in ERP helps in which of the following?

   a. Evaluating and responding to changing business conditions with accurate, timely financial data

   b. Easy compliance with financial reporting requirements

   c. Standardizing and streamlining operations

   d. **All of the above**

   e. None of the above

9. Gain from implementation of ERP results in which of the following?

   a. Improved business performance

   b. Improved decision making

   c. Increased ability to plan and grow

   d. **All of the above**

Sample Question Cards: Big Data

1. What is Big Data?

   a. Data about big things

   b. **Data which is extremely large in size (in petabytes)**

   c. Data about data

   d. None of the above

2. Which are not characteristics of Big Data?

    a. Volume

    b. Velocity

    c. **Virtuality**

    d. Variety

3. Which are key inputs for Big Data?

    a. Increased processing power

    b. Availability of tools and techniques for Big Data

    c. Increased storage capacities

    d. **All of the above**

4. Which are applications of Big Data?

    a. Targeted advertising

    b. Monitoring telecom network

    c. Customer sentiments

    d. **All of the above**

5. Which tools are used for Big Data?

    a. NoSQL

    b. MapReduce

    c. Hadoop Distributed File System

    d. **All of the above**

6. Social media and mobility are key contributors to Big Data: true or false?

    a. **True**

    b. False

7. Which is not a term related to Big Data?

    a. DatabasesMongoDB

    b. **Data Trigger**

    c. Pig

    d. SPARK

Illustrative Score Sheet for 3 teams with 20 Questions				
		Team A	Team B	Team C
	Original Bid	1200	2000	1300
Question Value				
100	Question-1	100	100	100
	Question-2	100	100	100
	Question-3	0	50	100
	Question-4	100	-50	50
	Question-5	0	50	100
	Question-6	100	100	100
	Question-7	50	50	-50
	Question-8	100	100	100
	Question-9	100	0	100
	Question-10	-50	50	-50
200	Question-11	200	200	0
	Question-12	100	200	200
	Question-13	-100	100	200
	Question-14	-100	100	0
	Question-15	200	200	-100
300	Question-16	300	300	300
	Question-17	150	-105	0
	Question-18	0	300	-150
	Question-19	-150	150	300
	Question-20	300	300	300
	SCORE	1500	2295	1700

Team B is declared winner due to high score and closer to original bid

Benefit Assessment

After consolidation of the learning, it's recommended to conduct a benefit assessment exercise to measure the gains from application of the game-based approach. The assessment could be in form of a written quiz on the subject with multiple-choice answers.

CHAPTER 4

■ ■ ■

Blindfold Game

Context: Understanding Essential Elements for Successful Teamwork

Collaboration is key to accomplishing a collective outcome; for instance, an IT program has many team members, and a team leader needs to foster collaboration and deliver the collective outcome. Teams are formed on the basis of individual skills needed for accomplishing the outcome and not necessarily on the basis of team members' ability to work in teams or their skills pertaining to basic aspects like goal setting, planning, communication, and trust; these aspects become critical to teamworking and collective success.

Collaborative work is essential across all organizations and needs attention to avoid factors such as overdependence on a dominant leader, lack of delegation, and so on. Collaborative work also allows these factors to be dealt with to improve collective effectiveness when teams intentionally focus on identifying and learning. It is normal to expect a leader to envision the final outcome and set out the plan to realize it. Engaging available resources to accomplish the plan and realize the vision involves multiple processes, for example defining the goals, planning resources, innovating within constraints of time, communicating, and steering progress. Each leader engages differently and so does each of the members in the team; this supports the entire journey of turning vision into reality.

Around 1999, I attended a leadership development program held outdoors. During the course of the program, we were made to play many competitive team-based games. One of such game was a leader guiding a blindfolded team to erect a tent made from cloth, sticks, and rope. Initially, we were all blindfolded and the leader was taken to the spot, at a different location, where material for the tent was placed. The leader was instructed that he couldn't give any clue or guidance to the team till they were at the spot, and he was also supposed to stay outside the work area; that is, during the activity of tent erection, he was supposed to provide only verbal guidance or instruction without physically participating himself. I was one of the blindfolded team members and our leader asked us to make a human chain and then he navigated us to the spot where we were to touch-'n'-feel, and under his guidance, work. Our team won this game with an extraordinary lead over competing teams. During analysis of the factors that contributed to winning, communication between leader and team members and among team members was identified as one of the key factors, since most of the members of

© Shreekant W Shiralkar 2016
S. W. Shiralkar, *IT Through Experiential Learning*, DOI 10.1007/978-1-4842-2421-2_4

the competing team chose to follow the leader's instructions and did not even discuss, inquire about, or challenge any of the instruction. The game had given me real-life experience about how communication has an extraordinary influence on teamwork and also about how team members play crucial roles in supporting leadership and contributing to the collective outcome.

Learning and experience from this game are at the core of the game that is explained in this chapter. The game simulates an environment that facilitates experiencing the factors that influence the outcome of a collective work. Examples of collective work include a software solution implementation program, an infrastructure project, or any teamwork in general that engages a large number of individuals as team members and is led by a program director or a project leader. The team bears responsibility for execution of the tasks, while the leader owns the responsibility for managing and achieving the envisioned outcome or end state.

The first time I had conceived this game was for an engagement in which I was assigned to deliver a training session on ERP to a group of very senior people belonging to a company that was embarking on an IT-led transformation by implementation of ERP. The activity was to facilitate identifying and understanding the critical success factors for the ERP program. The game generated the desired result. I later applied the core concept of the game in a variety of contexts and situations, for example to a class of students wanting to learn project management and to a group of CIO's in a management development program.

Let us now consider the procedure for the Blindfold Game (beginning with preparation, obtaining required materials) and how to conclude by examining the learnings from this game.

Activity

The Blindfold Game is a competitive team game. The game requires a good space, like a lecture hall with space for movement. Volunteers from the participants are invited to form two teams of four participants each and among them they are asked to choose their respective leaders. Both the teams are moved outside the hall so that the activity space is prepared for the game. Each of the team members is blindfolded outside the hall, and the activity space inside the hall is arranged with table, chairs, jug, and glasses in the center of the activity space. The leader of one of the teams is ushered in while the blindfolded team is kept outside. The leader is shown the arrangement of the table, chair, jug, and glasses, that he and his team needs to accomplish. The leader is then explained the rules of the game and specifically reminded that he or she cannot enter into the activity space and that he or she can't help any of the team members in the activity space. The table, chair, jug, and glasses arrangement is dismantled and these articles are moved to locations outside the activity space. Once leader signals his or her readiness, his or her team is ushered in and the timekeeper starts to measure the time. The blindfolded team members, under instructions of their leader, perform tasks assigned and accomplish the desired arrangement of the table, chairs, jug, and glasses; as they complete the arrangement, a timekeeper reports the time taken. The process repeats for the second team in the same sequence. After the second team accomplishes the arrangement, differences between the time taken and how the leaders and team performed are analyzed and learning is consolidated.

The game begins by moving both teams outside the hall. Then the leader of the first team is invited into the hall, and the instructor explains the task and rules (Figure 4-1).

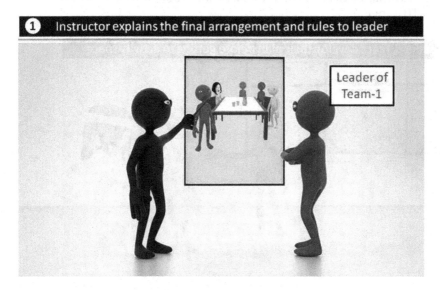

Figure 4-1. *Explanation of end state*

The members of the first team are blindfolded outside the hall (Figure 4-2).

Figure 4-2. *Team members blindfolded*

The members of the first team are helped move into the hall and handed over to the leader, and the instructor signals to start timing (which continues until the end state of the arrangement is accomplished). The leader starts sharing plans and tasks to be performed (Figure 4-3).

③ Leader & team develop their plan before getting to activity space

Figure 4-3. *Team leader explains the task to the team members.*

The team members begin performing the task while the leader guides progress and instructs from outside the activity space (Figure 4-4).

④ Team members start arranging articles within activity space

Figure 4-4. *Team members begin performing tasks.*

The team accomplishes part of the task under the leader's guidance (Figure 4-5).

Figure 4-5. Leader instructs and team performs

The timer is stopped as soon as the team completes the arrangement. Their blindfolds are then removed (Figure 4-6).

Figure 4-6. Blindfolds are removed after task is complete.

The same process is repeated with the second team. After the second team completes the task, the times are announced. The team that took less time is pronounced the winner.

The instructor now begins to record the experience—observations of the leaders, team members, and observers—to bring about learning from the experience (Figure 4-7).

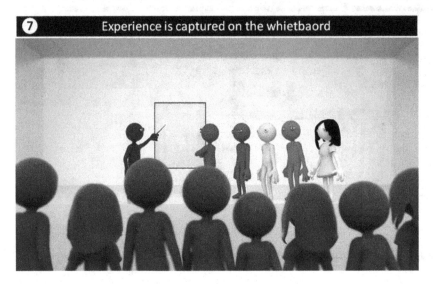

Figure 4-7. Experience and observations captured

An overview of the entire process is depicted in Figure 4-8.

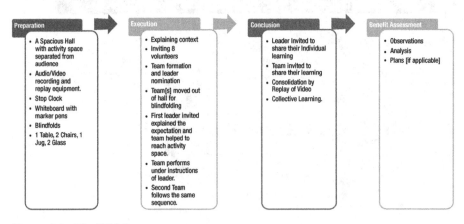

Figure 4-8. Blindfold Game

Process Flow

Complete details of the activities in the process flow are described in detail in the following sections.

Preparation

The game needs arrangement and preparation to ensure that learning is facilitated. The following arrangements and preparation are recommended:

1. The game needs a spacious hall that can accommodate an activity space that is unhindered by the observer sitting area; especially, the game area should be easy and safe for free movement of blindfolded people.

2. The activity space within the hall is segregated and identified specifically in such a way that all the observing participants are able to have direct visibility of the minutest movements as well as all communication that takes place among the team participants.

3. A sufficient number of blindfolds for team members who will participate in the game is needed. The blindfolded participants can be provided with helmets and safety equipment (if needed) to avoid any mishaps during the game.

4. A lightweight table with two lightweight chairs along with a plastic jug half-filled with water and two plastic glasses are required for the game. Each of these articles should be light, as they will be moved by blindfolded persons and are likely to cause problems if they are heavy or breakable.

5. A stopwatch for recording the time taken by the teams during the game is also needed.

6. Audio and video recording and playback arrangements are essential to facilitate the consolidation of learning, especially for the blindfolded participants; the audiovisual equipment should capture even the minutest movements and interactions during the Blindfold Game.

7. A whiteboard with marker pen is required for making notes during the game as well as during the learning consolidation phase.

8. Each participant should have notepad and pen to capture learning from observations.

Execution

Once all the preparation is complete, the game can begin.

Preactivity Briefing

One of the important factors for channeling learning from experience is to orient participants to the context; I recommend telling a relevant story before initiating them to the activity. In helping the participants relate to the context of leadership and teamwork, highlight how the leader has a vision of the end state or goal in mind, while team members usually have to be focused on executing the task at hand and most of the time do not focus on the outcome of the collective work.

1. Invite eight volunteers to play the game.

2. Help the volunteers to form two teams and facilitate nomination of a leader within each of the teams.

3. Name the two teams and create their scoring charts on one of the whiteboards.

4. Request all other participants (i.e., observers) to be extremely observant of and sensitive to each and every element of the experience they will observe and to note these observations in their notepads. The request to keep mental notes on the experience is stressed upon for the two leaders and the team members.

5. Caution all the observing participants about maintaining absolute silence while two teams compete with each other in the activity space.

Activity

1. Send both teams out of the hall so that they will not be able to discern the configuration of material in the activity space.

2. Arrange the articles (table, chairs, jugs, and glasses) in their desired state in middle of the activity space. See Figure 4-9.

Figure 4-9. *End state of arrangement*

3. Now nominate volunteers for performing the following:

   - A timekeeper job to run the stopwatch.

   - A monitor to ensure that blindfolding for the team members is done properly and that there has been no prior preparation or planning by either of the teams. The monitor also helps the blindfolded participants during their movement from outside to the activity space inside the hall and ensures the safety of blindfolded participants in general.

4. Invite one of the team leaders inside the hall and show the end state of the table, chairs, jug, and glasses in the middle of the activity space.

5. Explain following rules to the leader:

   - The leader cannot physically perform any of the tasks.

   - The leader can choose any language or verbal means to communicate with the team members.

   - The leader can formulate a strategy for ensuring completion of the desired state.

6. Once the leader acknowledges readiness to start the game, dismantle the end state and keep articles outside of the activity space so that it will be necessary for team members to move them into the desired arrangement state (Figure 4-10).

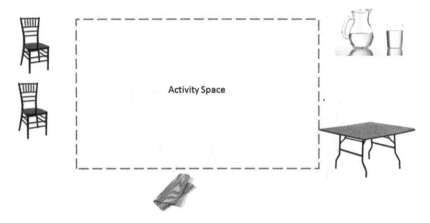

Figure 4-10. *Initial state of articles to be arranged*

7. Advise the monitor to get the team members into the hall and hand them over to the leader and signal to the timekeeper to start the stopwatch.

8. Ensure that audio/video recording equipment records each of the activities being performed by the team in the game.

9. The leader starts guiding team members with tasks; once the desired arrangement state is accomplished, check with the timekeeper and record the elapsed time on the whiteboard.

10. Blindfolds of the performing team members are removed, and each of them (including the leader) is asked to record their experiences while accomplishing the task. This should be done without any discussion among themselves or with other participants.

11. Now, before the activity is repeated by the second team under identical conditions, observers are specially advised to record their observations on what made the difference between the two teams in achieving the end state.

12. The leader of the second team is invited to the activity space and given the same instructions that were given to the first leader, and then the second team is invited to the activity space to perform the task under the same conditions as for the first one.

13. After completion of the activity by the second group, the time taken is recorded on the whiteboard.

14. After removing the blindfolds, advise each of them (including the leader) to record their experiences while accomplishing the task.

Once the game is over, observations from experience are collected and crystallized in learning in the concluding section.

Conclusion

The difference in the times needed by the teams, form the basic premise, to start collecting observations and analysis for the purpose of generating learning on essential elements for successful teamwork. The recommended process to capture learning from the experience is as follows:

1. Use the second whiteboard to start recording the elements of learning.

2. Invite the leader of the losing team to share learnings, which are captured on the whiteboard; the process is repeated with the leader of the winning team.

3. The process of capturing learning is now repeated for each of the team members from both the teams.

Each of the observer participants is requested to read out loud from his/her notepad and share the top three learnings from the experience. Generally, most learnings are captured early, and participants may repeat many; these repeated learnings should be identified by additional checkmarks next to them. That helps to distinguish more critical learnings from less critical ones (Figure 4-11).

Figure 4-11. *Instructor consolidating collective learning*

In my experience, learnings differ among groups, since the groups may be composed of anyone from managers in a corporate environment to college students. However, certain elements remain the same, since factors influencing teamwork do not change; only their intensities differ depending on context and environment.

Facilitate participants' choice of words; for example, interactivity among team members, instructions from the leader, and discussion between team members and the leader all would be identified under a common theme of *"communication,"* whether it's about the quantum of communication or the choice of words or sequence of instructions.

The recorded video is replayed for identifying missing observations and learnings, if any. The replay also helps reinforce and consolidate learnings that were experienced and collected on the whiteboard. Here are sample learning themes that I encountered across most of the sessions:

- Leadership style has huge impact on teamwork.

- Team engagement is essential for success of teamwork.

- Communication is critical aspect of a successful teamwork.

- Planning is essential to successfully accomplish a teamwork.

- Coordination between team members as well as with leader and team member is pivotal in successful teamwork.

- Leader has to maintain a balance of delegation and control for successful teamwork.

- Team members' capability to understand the big-picture while performing his/her task plays crucial role in successful teamwork.

- Trust between team is essential element for success of teamwork.

- Passion demonstrated by leader and team enhances the probability of success of a teamwork.

After consolidation of the learning, it's recommended to summarize the observations, and if applicable, track and monitor the gains from application of the gamification.

Sample: Summary Observations

The hallmark of successful teamwork is that the leader is able to get things done and deliver on time and within budget by getting best outcomes from the energy and efforts of team. These successful leaders have common characteristics, and here's a quick list from my experience:

- Illustrates and quantifies the strategy

- Communicates effectively

- Creates an environment that fosters each team member to contribute to the success of the collective outcome

- Uses a participatory decision-making process

- Masters the "operational art"

- Provides timely alerts as well as rewards and encouragement to the team members

- Knows the difference between boldness and recklessness

Benefit Assessment

After consolidation of the learning, it's recommended to conduct a benefit assessment exercise to measure the gains from application of the game-based approach. Here are some of the recommended assessment methods:

1. Stakeholder feedback: Team members, peers, and supervisors could be surveyed for feedback about a participant. Many organizations regularly measure employee engagement; a positive change in employee engagement would be another measure of success. Human resource units can measure interpersonal conflict trends. Customer feedback is another measure of how team functioning has improved: "customer" here refers to both direct beneficiaries of the team outcomes (e.g., for a large IT program, the program director is the direct beneficiary of the individual project teams) and indirect beneficiaries (e.g., the CIO of the client company for the IT program being delivered by a service delivery vendor).

2. Results: Measure impact on real-world production; for example for an IT project, it would be defect level, on-time delivery, on-budget delivery, and so on.

CHAPTER 5

■ ■ ■

Arrangement Game

Context: Understanding Impact of Competing Constraints in Teamwork

Achieving a perfect balance between mutually competing and diverse demands is a myth; for example, having a good stock of inventory to achieve the highest level of customer service has to trade off with impact on the cost of carrying inventory. Situations having a diverse set of demands therefore create a dynamic environment where each participant has to switch plans and priorities and give importance to the outcome of teamwork.

Let me elaborate on the situation with an example of a sales manager having key responsibility for customer service. In this role, he is expected to raise the inventory of products as high as possible. On the other hand, however, the warehouse manager, responsible for reducing the cost of carrying inventory, is expected to maintain the lowest possible inventory of products. In this situation, unless both the role holders review their responsibilities and priorities, jointly with other stakeholders of the organization, the organization is likely to suffer, due to either loss of sales or higher cost of inventory.

A similar situation is created during any transformational program. For example, during an ERP implementation, the key users from the business, with primary focus on carrying out their routine business tasks and functions, most likely do not attribute enough importance to the quality of inputs being given for the design of an IT solution. Failure to get quality input by a software consultant designing the IT solution directly impacts the overall quality of the IT solution, ultimately impacting the business efficiency in the future.

By creating an environment that facilitates experiencing the impact of mutually competing expectations on the collective outcome, a higher probability of success for the collective outcome may be generated. For example, in the above-described scenario of implementation of an ERP solution, the program is more likely to generate intended outcomes when executives from business functions provide quality inputs during the design of the ERP solution.

This is the premise of the learning game explained in this chapter. The game simulates and enables experiencing a dynamic environment for a group of participants and the impact on the collective outcome, due to varied plans and expectations. Participants are expected to keep focus on their individual objectives as well as the team's goal.

© Shreekant W Shiralkar 2016
S. W. Shiralkar, *IT Through Experiential Learning*, DOI 10.1007/978-1-4842-2421-2_5

I conceived the "Arrangement Game" for an engagement when I was assigned to deliver a session on ERP, to an organization, that was embarking on an IT transformation led by implementation of ERP. The group of managers from the organization represented diverse set of functions and roles, such as sales manager, head of manufacturing, finance manager, and human resource manager. The game facilitated bringing about their collective understanding of the diversity of expectations from the intended ERP program. Later I leveraged the game for a variety of contexts and situations: for example, a class of students from postgraduate class of a management institute studying project management, as well as a group of managers in a management development program for increasing appreciation of the impact of stakeholder dynamics.

The game is played as a competition between two teams of nine participants each. The game is played in a room having two grids of 2'×2' tiles (nine tiles per grid, for a total of 18 tiles), drawn/visible on the floor. The teams have to arrange themselves on the grid in the specific arrangement (Figures 5-1 and 5-2). The objective of the game is to make an arrangement such that each person on the team has to be at a distance of exactly one arm's length from any other person, and each person has to be within the grid standing on one of the tiles maintaining the same arm's-length distance from two people that he/she had selected before the start of the game. The arrangement is therefore determined partly by each of the team members and partly by the dynamic environment within the group. Each person is allotted a number (which is prominently displayed on a preprinted number tag [a.k.a. badge] worn by that person), and every person also picks two other numbers within the range of 1 to 9 and writes them on a piece of paper, which is then put in his or her pocket. These two "pocketed" numbers are not disclosed to anyone; they represent individual priorities or aspirations hidden from other team members and therefore represent the root cause of the dynamic state of the whole team. Teams have to achieve the desired arrangement within 5 minutes.

Competition with the other team in the Arrangement Game creates an element of urgency, accelerating the learning process. The objective of the game is to learn about the impact of individual goals on the collective unit (e.g., making the most of possibilities offered by new technology for business process efficiency); such individual goals might include a focus on technology or business function, for example. The dynamic nature of the game keeps the learning fun-filled, stress-free, and interesting.

Arrangement Game

The Arrangement Game is to be played by each of the participants attending the learning workshop up to a maximum of 18 people in two teams of nine members each. The group is divided into two teams, and their goals are (a) to accomplish a perfect arrangement within the allotted time and (b) to win by doing so in less time than the other team. "Perfect arrangement" here refers to formation of the team in such a way that each of the nine participants is at arm's length from the two other selected team members at arm's length and occupying one tile in the grid.

There are two limiting factors for a team: the constraint of time (5 minutes) and the time taken to accomplish arrangement by the other team.

So, in order to win, a team has to finish not only within 5 minutes but also earlier than the other team. The game concludes when either of the teams has arranged itself in the expected formation or after 5 minutes, whichever comes first.

Figure 5-1 shows teams standing on grids in the activity space. Figure 5-2 will help you visualize the Arrangement Game.

The two teams stand on either side of the instructor. Initially, they stand in free form and as soon as the instructor signals the start of the game they start to arrange themselves on the grid on the floor. Each team member also checks for the arm's-length distance by extending his or her arms to the shoulders of the people to the front and to the side.

Figure 5-1. Teams standing on grid in activity space

After 5 minutes, the instructor asks the teams to stop movements. The instructor then starts measuring the teams' scores on the basis of the correlation between the "pocketed" numbers and the allotted numbers on the tags of the people at arm's length. Each participant satisfying the conditions of the arrangement (i.e., the participant is one arm's length from the two correct teammates) is given one point, and this is recorded on the scoreboard.

Figure 5-2. *Arrangement accomplished within time limit*

In my experience, the perfect arrangement is never accomplished, since the proximity requirement based on the undisclosed selection of two numbers by each participant creates inherent incompatibilities; rather, the team keeps churning around in constant movement. The team having the most members achieving their desired arrangement is declared the winner.

Let us now examine the task-level details of the Arrangement Game beginning with preparation, prerequisite material, and then the process for its execution including steps to consolidate learning after its conclusion.

An overview of the entire game is depicted in the process flow shown in Figure 5-3.

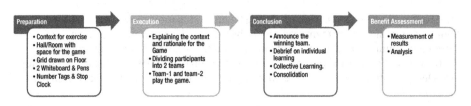

Figure 5-3. *Arrangement Game process flow*

Complete details of the activities in the process flow are described in the following sections.

Preparation

The Arrangement Game needs preparation that includes the following:

1. A spacious hall with a large floor that allows free movement of participants while playing the game.

2. Drawing two grids with nine squares each in the floor of the space where the participants will play the game. The tile size within the grid should be large enough to allow a person stand easily. I recommend tiles of about 2′×2′.

3. Create number tags from 1 to 9 in both team colors (e.g., Green and Blue) with strings for participants to wear and display prominently on their torsos, both front and back.

4. 36 papers for participants to use for writing their undisclosed chosen numbers (two per participant).

5. A stopwatch to measure the time taken by teams to accomplish the arrangement.

6. A whiteboard with marker to display time taken by each of the teams.

7. Whiteboards and markers to capture collective learning notes and consolidate learning.

8. Notepads and pens for the observing participants (i.e., participants who are not playing the game).

9. A placeholder like a whiteboard for display of the rules of the game that participants can refer to before and during the game.

Rules

1. Each team has a time limit of 5 minutes to finish the arrangement.

2. The winning team is chosen on the basis of having the greater number of members achieving their goals within 5 minutes.

3. The members have to be at arm's length from each other, standing on a tile within the grid on the floor.

Execution

Once all the preparation is complete, the game can begin.

Preactivity Briefing

Introduce participants to the session by relating the upcoming game to the context of dealing with mutually competing and diverse sets of demands, along with extremely routine references to examples like having one's cake and eating it too or getting the best work from people with low salary expectations. While they are part of an ecosystem that has an expectation of collective balance and/or optimal solutions to problems.

To ensure that participants experience the game in the applicable scenario and develop a collective learning, a good amount of time needs to be spent in contextualizing the exercise before introducing them to the actual game. Please note that in absence of contextualization, the game is less likely to generate the intended learnings. The following are examples of contextualization.

For an ERP-led transformation program: identifying two mutually challenging factors; running the business function without disruption or needing to take the time to provide quality input to the consultants designing the ERP solution. Similarly, for a project management program: identifying challenges in producing deliverables on time and yet with the expected cost and quality.

After context setting, the game can begin.

Activity

1. Invite 18 volunteers from the participants and get them to the activity space where the ground has the two grids of nine tiles each.

2. Make the 18 volunteers stand in a row and create two teams on the basis of counting off by twos or every alternate person.

3. Distribute the number badges from 1 to 9 randomly among the team members and ask everyone to wear or display them uniformly.

4. Give each of the participants two paper slips and instruct him/her to write any two numbers between 1 and 9. These two numbers need to be different from than the number on his/her badge and cannot be disclosed to any teammate.

5. The instructor records each participant's badge number on both of that participant's paper slips (in top right corner) and then gives it back to the participant to be kept by him/her hidden from other team members.

6. Request all the other participants to be extremely sensitive to each and every element of the experience they will undergo, be it as observer, leader, or team member, and to make a note of these experiences in their notepad.

7. Nominate a timekeeper to use stopwatch and announce duration.

8. Caution all the participants about maintaining absolute silence while people are performing in the activity space.

9. Now ask them to be ready for the activity while requesting timekeeper for readiness with the stopwatch.

10. Announce to the group that you expect them to have an arrangement of the entire group in such a way that

    a. Each of the team members is occupying one tile of the grid.

    b. He/she is at arm's length from the other team members representing the two numbers he/she wrote on his/her paper slips.

    c. These two team members may be on any adjacent tile.

11. Now advise the participants that they have 5 minutes to move and create an arrangement such that each one accomplishes his or her objective and the group collectively also accomplishes a formation that satisfies the rules of the arrangement.

12. Announce the start, with the timekeeper keeping note of time elapsed.

13. At the close of 5 minutes, announce completion of the time and advise each participant to stay wherever they are on the grid.

14. Compare the position of each participant on the grid and the positions of the two other team members which he/she desired to be on adjacent tile and at arm's length.

15. For each individual arrangement that met the rule, record one point on the whiteboard.

16. Announce the winning team on the basis of higher score.

Once the game is over, observations from experience are collected and crystallized in learning in the concluding section.

Debrief

The difference in time needed by the teams is the basic premise to start the debrief process to identify learning from the experience.

1. Invite each of the participants to share one key learning from the experience.

2. Use the second whiteboard to start recording the elements of learning.

3. A learning that is repeated within the participants is given an additional checkmark.

4. Facilitate participants in their choice of words. For example,

   a. Interactivity between team members or

   b. Discussion between team members

Each word (i.e., interactivity, instructions, and discussion) would be identified under a common theme of "communication," whether it's about the quantum of communication, the choice of words, or the sequence of instructions.

5. Figure 5-4 and the following list provide the suggested learning themes that I encountered across a large number of performances of this exercise:

   a. Awareness of mutual expectations helps

   b. Teamwork is essential for collective gains

   c. Communication is critical

   d. Planning always helps

   e. Coordination is necessary

Figure 5-4. *Instructor consolidating collective learning*

In my experience, learning for one group differs from that for other due to differences in their corporate environments. However, key learning themes remain the same as factors influencing teamwork do not change: only their intensity differs.

The hallmark of successful teamwork is that each individual is able to appreciate the impact of individual actions and expectations on the collective outcome. The successful teams have following common characteristics:

1. Higher priority assigned to collective outcome than to individual outcomes.

2. Cohesive and aligned team delivers results early.

3. Regular and open communication across team provides for better coordination and positive effect on collective outcome.

4. Plan before execution for better outcomes.

5. Effective coordination within and across team is an essential element for successful outcome.

49

After consolidation of the learning, it's recommended to conduct a benefit assessment exercise to track and monitor the gains from application of the gamification.

Benefit Assessment

The understanding participants have developed during the game will begin to show its impact in improved collective outcomes and also in reduced conflict levels in dealing with competing constraints. Reduction in the number of iterations of IT requirements for the business function can be another measure, as increased understanding of mutual constraints will directly reduce such iterations.

CHAPTER 6

■ ■ ■

Treasure Hunt

Context: Rapid Adoption of New Technology

The past two decades have been truly disruptive to the business environment and have brought about a large-scale change. We all know that technological innovations like Internet, social media, and cloud computing have been the cause of completely new business models; for example, one of the most popular social media, Facebook, does not create its content, and Uber, the largest taxi operator in the world, doesn't own taxis or employ drivers. Furthermore, these innovative business models have developed in an extremely short time. This rapidly changing environment has created a need for change in existing business processes to constantly adapt to changing models. It's therefore no surprise that enterprise in today's world is identified and differentiated on the basis of its innovative capital and people instead of other attributes like its location or physical infrastructure, as was the case in the earlier environment.

Resistance to change is human nature, and therefore changes forced by the business environment are not welcomed by the employees of any organization. The need to adopt new technology and transform, to stay current and beat the competition is encountered by all sizes and types of organizations. Adoption of new technology and/or changes to the business processes make it essential for the employees to learn and adapt at the pace of change; that is, the situation causes a fast-paced learning for the employees. The situation therefore poses a real challenge for organizations that need to survive and compete. The intensity and impact of the challenge are higher for large organizations having workforces spread across different geographic locations, from different cultures, and with different levels of learning interest and ability.

During my assignment at a very large state-owned oil company that had embraced a strategy for IT-led transformation, the strategy was aimed at generating agility in enterprise and business processes, enabling real-time information for faster decision making and a quicker response to the customer. I was part of the core team that was engaged in designing and implementing an enterprise-wide transformation program through aggressive use of IT. A critical factor in the success of this strategy and program hinged on early adoption of technology by a large number of employees in an extremely short period of time and more so by the decision makers, who were more resistant to change than the younger workforce. Resistance to the incident change was very visible and posed a huge risk to the success of the transformation program. The challenge was similar at a global software service delivery organization that needed to bring in change in the processes and adoption of a state-of-the-art knowledge management platform.

© Shreekant W Shiralkar 2016
S. W. Shiralkar, *IT Through Experiential Learning*, DOI 10.1007/978-1-4842-2421-2_6

The change was intended to produce competitive advantages of cost and quality in their service delivery from India. In both of these situations, I generated outcomes in terms of rapid adoption by application of a game-based approach premised on experiential learning. I had conceptualized and deployed a virtual Treasure Hunt (VTH) that used a combination of game and competition. The Treasure Hunt facilitated rapid propagation of awareness as well as learning new technology.

Treasure Hunts and competition are known to have natural and instinctive attraction among people, and a combination of these therefore provides the most appropriate channel to generate a compelling theme for adopting new technology or new process. As you know, Treasure Hunt is a game having many players competing to find hidden articles, locations, or places by using a series of clues. The game of Treasure Hunt is usually an indoor or outdoor activity where the treasure could be located anywhere in the area. A VTH is a digitized version of the game, transposed into the electronic medium, where participants follow clues and visit different web pages (or even physical locations) to solve riddles sequentially and win prizes to succeed in the Treasure Hunt.

The VTH ensured an accelerated adoption of a completely new decision support system for this very large oil company, which had a diverse and geographically spread workforce. I was able to demonstrate the impact of the idea by rapid increase in usage of the new system. The impact was equally outstanding for a multinational software service delivery organization in transforming the knowledge management platform and ensuring its exponential adoption in an extremely short period of time.

Having discussed the background and gains from deploying the VTH for rapid adoption of technology and process change, I will now provide detailed design guidelines and explanations that will help you to deploy the VTH for bringing about rapid adoption of technology and/or change of process.

Virtual Treasure Hunt

A Treasure Hunt game begins with decoding a set of clues that lead to the treasure. VTH transposes the game into the computing environment where the participant needs to solve a puzzle to get the next clue in the sequence, ultimately concluding the game with finding the treasure. The game is played by all the participants, who move from one stage to the next on the basis of solving puzzles with the aid of clues. The game concludes after the participant is able to move to the final stage and discover the hidden treasure. All the while, participants are competing to see who moves the fastest.

In designing the VTH, elements of competition and exploration form the core theme. The competitive aspect triggers speed, the game element induces interest without force or pressure, and finally exploration facilitates coverage of the subject— for instance, technical nuances and features offered by new technology and/or new process, channelling an accelerated adoption of new technology and/or process. To design exploration of new technology and/or process, ensure that the pace of learning is accelerated gradually and that learning begins with basic aspects, moving on to advanced and then to complex in sequence. In designing the sequence, care has to be exercised in separating basic and must-learn aspects from nice-to-know types, and design should ensure that learning of basic and must-learn ones is accomplished while providing for nice-to-know types based on the interest and appetite of the participants. Design the sequence in such a way that initially the participant needs to spend less time on learning new technology and is drawn toward the game and competition, while later parts of sequence ensure that the participant spends more time in exploration and applies himself to strategizing learning for winning and staying ahead of competition.

The figures in this chapter will help you visualize the experience created for Treasure Hunt participants. In Figure 6-1, two participants log on to the Treasure Hunt application using the link published via enterprise portal and register as participants after accepting the rules and regulations of the game.

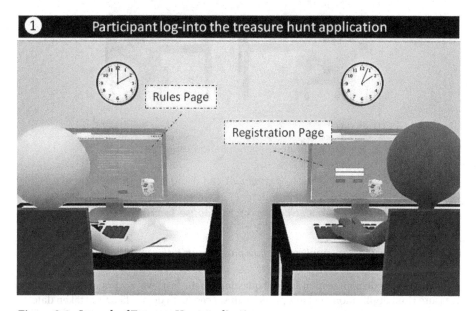

Figure 6-1. *Launch of Treasure Hunt application*

Treasure Hunt begins with multiple-choice questions on new technology. By correctly responding, the participant moves to the next level, which has similar questions but of higher complexity. The process engages the participant to use the clue hyperlinks, which lead to documentation on new technology or the software solution itself. The participant responds after learning the correct response (Figure 6-2).

53

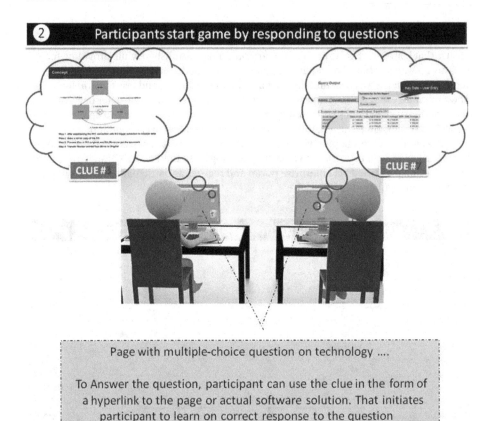

Figure 6-2. Treasure Hunt application pulls participants into new technology.

After the participant responds to all questions of the last level accurately, the Treasure Hunt application declares participant success with details like time taken date completed, and so on: for example, the "CONGRATULATIONS YOU HAVE FOUND TREASURE" notification, and a clock in corner of the computer screen to show total time taken (Figure 6-3).

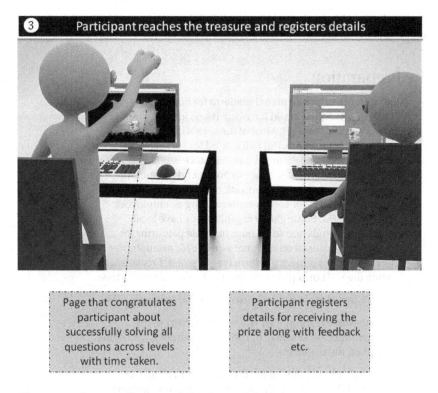

Figure 6-3. Treasure Hunt completion by participants

The objective of accomplishing the rapid adoption of technology and/or new process necessitates a short duration of the overall VTH. Having a high level of participation in a short span of time also requires support of an internal communications campaign that ensures immediate awareness. It is therefore of paramount importance that a communication plan for creating instant awareness is part of the design and preparation.

Let us now examine the task-level details of the VTH beginning with preparation and prerequisite material and then the process for its execution, including steps to consolidate learning after the conclusion. An overview of the entire game is depicted in Figure 6-4.

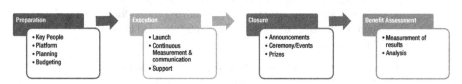

Figure 6-4. Treasure Hunt process flow

Complete details of the activities in the process flow are described in detail in the following sections.

Activity Preparation

1. Platform: Identify the internal platform for hosting the VTH. This platform should have provisions for designing and developing the VTH. Most of the organizations today have an intralink web portal that is used for serving as the single window for all digitized internal processes as well as sharing information like change in policy and updates on developments across the organization. The internal portal is also the platform for collaboration among all employees across the world. Some global organizations have local community portals and some have multiple platforms for collaboration focused on different aspects; for example, the knowledge management platform is segregated. I recommend hosting the VTH on a platform with the following parameters:

    a. One that is most regularly used by the target employees.

    b. One where hosting VTH will not hinder any of the organization's sensitive or confidential aspects also being run on the platform.

    c. One that has technical features to support all aspects of the VTH, for example, the ability to capture the time taken to crack the clues, and the ability to provide hyperlink access to the technical system and/or new process which is the core objective of learning.

2. The team that is designing the VTH needs high participation and involvement of the experts in the new technology or process being introduced. The role holders like subject matter experts and/or process owner should be part of the design process. These experts will help in all the important aspects of the VTH. Following are the high-level expectations from experts:

    a. Identification of all the must-learn and nice-to-know aspects about the new technology and/or process for a comprehensive coverage of all aspects that need to be adopted by the participants.

    b. Linkage of the specific aspect on new technology and/or process to the best learning material about it.

    c. Segregation of each aspect for design of different stages of the Treasure Hunt i.e. simple to complex, must-know to nice-to-know etc.

3. To ensure that participants don't lose interest in playing and drop out midway, each of the stages or levels of the VTH should be designed differently (e.g., initially it could begin with just a few easy multiple-choice answers and proceed to tougher puzzles in later stages). The first few sets of questions or puzzles describe basic aspects of technology or the new process that are well known. The next questions or puzzles should make the participant either use the new technology or read about the new process, and still-further sets of questions or puzzles should require more knowledge about the technology or process, and so on.

4. Design the game so that most participants will easily qualify and be able to play to some level without much effort or preparation.

5. Rewarding early successes for each participant will help more people stay engaged over meeting tougher entry criteria. However, the concluding stages need to be tough to ensure only a few reach the treasure giving the sense of winning to those reaching it earlier than rest.

6. The final stage or some stages before the final should be dynamic (i.e., depending on context of the participant the puzzles could vary; however, the level of toughness should not vary).

7. Create an internal communication campaign that ensures awareness about VTH well before it is actually launched. The communication campaign needs to use all the channels that help in instant awareness among all employees. Messaging across channels will need to be designed differently; for example, mobile text messages and messages over official e-mail will be of one type, whereas stickers, display banners, and standees will be of another type. Further, each phase of the overall campaign will need different messaging. I also recommend choosing a campaign theme or title that defines the objective for the VTH. The title should be appealing enough to generate attention from each intended employee.

Materials and Resources:

1. VTH application development team for design and testing of the VTH on the Intranet/enterprise platform. Team of web developers for enabling the VTH.

2. Well-defined objective questions on the new technology and/or the process being introduced. The language of each question needs to be simple and easy and generally understood by all, without scope for confusion or different interpretations. Using rhyme, humor, and figurative language

is recommended, and to make it interesting the clues should be in a multimedia format. The questions and their correct responses need to be classed according to their scope and complexity, which will help in deciding the VTH stage in which they should be placed.

3. Well-defined rules for the VTH are essential. They will help to avoid grievances or conflicts among participants, and most important they will help to avoid any possibility of loss of interest on the part of the participants.

4. Set of FAQ to respond to questions like "How many attempts can I make?" or "How do I know my score?"

5. Means to monitor and measure participation statistics. I would also recommend having a measure of the current state of use of new technology and/or process as baseline for an accurate feel for the outcome from the application of the VTH and its effectiveness.

6. Necessary infrastructure for the physical part of the awareness campaign along with well-defined process for communication across stake holders. While examples of electronic mode are e-mail, text messages, alerts on internal communication channel, and so on, I have listed below examples of the infrastructure for the physical part of the awareness campaign:

   a. Employee notice boards.

   b. Display banners for multiple stages of the event.

   c. Identified display locations for display of banners like entrance and exits, reception area of each office, notice boards in elevators, lunch room or cafeteria within offices.

7. Prizes and rewards that prompt competition such as a winner's trophy, gifts, and tokens of appreciation across many categories. Recognizing every participant will support higher participation and ensure accomplishment of the intended objective(s). While recognition could be attractive enough, higher-level prizes or rewards should be progressively more appealing and reduced in numbers for maintaining the spirit of competition.

Sample Wireframe for Treasure Hunt

The web pages for the VTH play an important role in pulling attention and continued interest in playing the game. The link to the Treasure Hunt should lead to its microsite within the intralink/enterprise platform; the following are sample pages that provide the basic idea.

The login page is recommended to provide just formal registration for the participant (Figure 6-5). The page could be a form with a few more details as necessitated by the purpose. This page will enable user to log in using EnterpriseID/password. I had also created a logo-like image that represented the Treasure Hunt, and each and every webpage had this image.

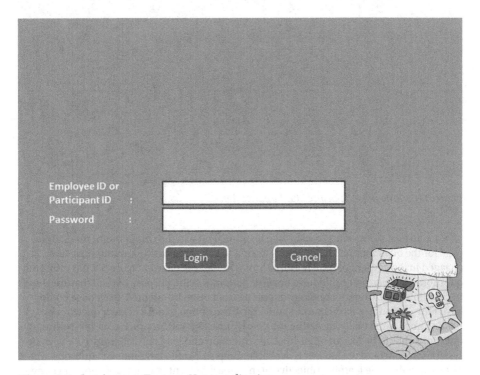

Figure 6-5. *Log-in page: Treasure Hunt application*

The rules page (Figure 6-6) should be the first page after registration so that each participant understands and accepts the rules before starting the activity.

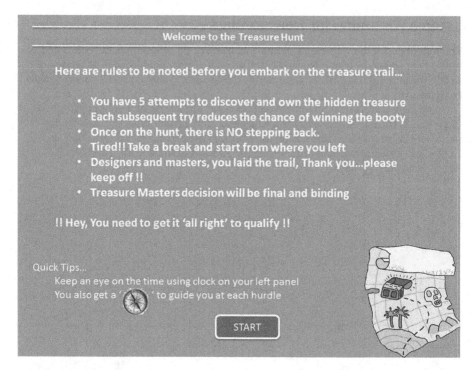

Welcome to the Treasure Hunt

Here are rules to be noted before you embark on the treasure trail...

- You have 5 attempts to discover and own the hidden treasure
- Each subsequent try reduces the chance of winning the booty
- Once on the hunt, there is NO stepping back.
- Tired!! Take a break and start from where you left
- Designers and masters, you laid the trail, Thank you...please keep off !!
- Treasure Masters decision will be final and binding

!! Hey, You need to get it 'all right' to qualify !!

Quick Tips...
Keep an eye on the time using clock on your left panel
You also get a '   ' to guide you at each hurdle

START

Figure 6-6. *Rule page: Treasure Hunt application*

To create a sense of urgency to take less time and win the competition, the sample page for the questions will have a clock ticking to keep the participants attentive and engaged in the content of the Treasure Hunt. The sample page in Figure 6-7 has only one question; however, you could have more depending on the purpose of the Treasure Hunt. In case there many new technology or process aspects to be adopted, each page could have more questions. Participants should have the option to answer each question by reading about or actually accessing the new technology and/or process; in this regard, the questions should be like an open-book examination and lead participants to the page or system screen where the answer is available. Help and guide links for each question will ensure that the core learning objective of the Treasure Hunt (e.g., instant adoption of new technology or new process) is accomplished, as these links will allow participants to read or browse information.

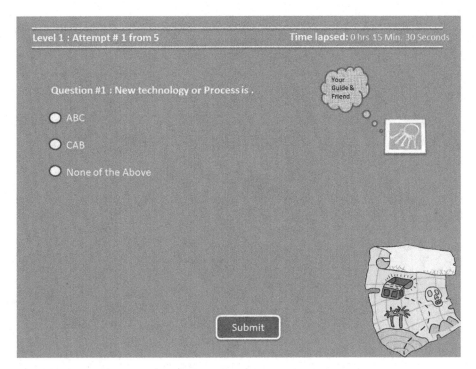

Figure 6-7. *Quiz page: Treasure Hunt application*

Once a participant submits correct responses to the first set of questions, the sample page (Figure 6-8) for level completion should provide feedback to the participant on accomplishment and elapsed time thus far, as well as an invitation to enter the next level.

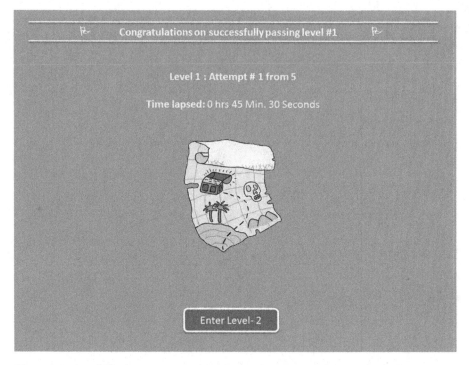

Figure 6-8. *Level change page: Treasure Hunt application*

Eventually, the participant will pass the final level and reach the concluding page, such as that shown in Figure 6-9. This could have a greeting message along with the statistics of accomplishment.

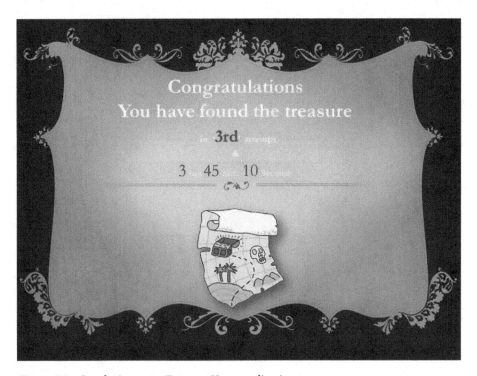

Figure 6-9. *Conclusion page: Treasure Hunt application*

An additional sample page (Figure 6-10) could be inserted at appropriate stages of the Treasure Hunt (e.g., for being first-day participants, for people crossing level 1, and so on) to collect details from the participants.

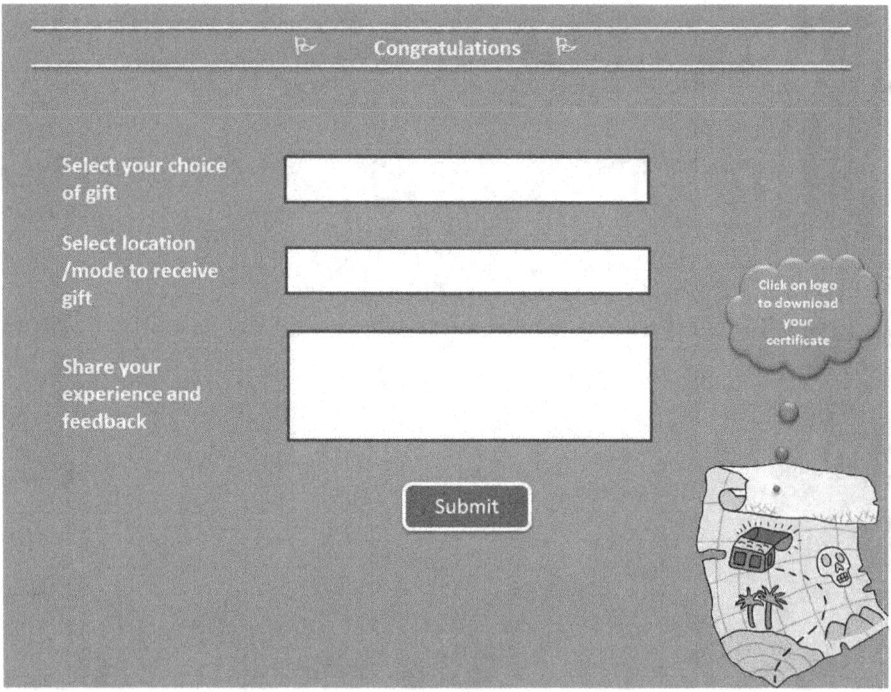

Figure 6-10. Winners page: Treasure Hunt application

Execution

Now that all the preparation is complete, execution of the game can begin as explained in this section.

Preactivity Awareness Campaign

Accomplishing early adoption of technology and/or new process in the shortest possible time necessitates an awareness campaign that will have widespread coverage, and almost all employees will get to know about the VTH.

Instant awareness by use of physical infrastructure is necessary. Use of employee notice boards, banners at key spots like entrance and exits, standees near the reception area of each office, and appropriate material to create awareness at elevators and canteen areas are some examples to cause instant awareness about VTH (Figures 6-11 through 6-13). Posters and standees should be placed at various attention-getting locations throughout the organization's offices.

Figure 6-11. *Sample standee for creating awareness*

Figure 6-12. *Sample notice board sticker for creating awareness*

65

Figure 6-13. *Sample banner for awareness campaign*

The awareness can also be complemented by usage of pop-up messages on intralink/enterprise portal, announcements through messaging systems (if any), and e-mail messages. To ensure getting desired attention from each of the target employee and in the time-frame of the VTH, it is also essential that the visuals are designed in compelling looks and appeal. I would recommend using a logo-type image to consolidate the visual "brand" of the Treasure Hunt.

The awareness campaign needs to run through the entire period of the Treasure Hunt to sustain the level of engagement. A sustained and active engagement is essential to accomplishing the core objective of Treasure Hunt. An example could be displaying the level of participation (with key participants and their accomplishments) over intralink and other channels of awareness (Figure 6-14).

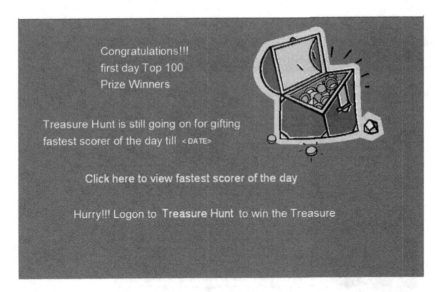

Figure 6-14. Sample message to invite participation

Closure

Once the Treasure Hunt is concluded, feedback from participants and the stakeholders is collected. The process could be online or a well-identified matrix (e.g., change in level of new requirements from technology or reduced use of the legacy technology, etc.). Such measures are collected and reported in a conclusion note that acknowledge the outcomes, thanks the contributors, and establishes the returns on investment that was made in the whole activity. A sample note is reproduced in Figure 6-15.

Virtual Treasure Hunt - An innovative idea to increase awareness

Team launched a virtual Treasure hunt in February end with the aim of increasing awareness and image.... The hugely popular event saw a soaring hit rate of the site, thus living up to its purpose

Recent developments triggered the necessity to increase awareness of NEW TECHNOLOGY which is enabling the organization with competitive edge and a vast knowledge universe. With this as the backdrop – the idea of Virtual Treasure Hunt was conceived. The two week event (27th feb – 13th March) saw a flurry of pre-event activities with specialized teams set up for work distribution. Close coordination within the team helped achieve smooth execution of the event, though at time leaving furried eyebrows in the execution team.

As March 26th dawned, the execution team was ready with its posters and standees to be placed at various strategic locations across the country. Teasers were dispatched to give a heads up to the community. Last minute issues with standees was sorted out quickly to prevent any setbacks to the event.

Friday - March 27th was the D-day for the execution team who had laboured so hard to get everything in place. The link was activated at midnight of March 26ths and the very first hit was received at 2:40 AM IST. Seemingly people were waiting for the link to get active and thus the event went rolling like there is no stop. Over the next 2 weeks, execution teams day started with questions like "How many attempts till now?" and ended with "What is today's hit count?" By March 13th, more than 16,500 trails had been blazed in search of the 'elusive' treasure.

Pat in the back came through acknowledgments of the leadership team for the event. So while Managing Director referred to Treasure hunt as "an innovative idea that we applied in our work!!" in his town hall at Detroit, Hongkong, Perth and lauded the able leadership of Shreekar and Shirakar and the team effort that went in. A note of appreciation from Global Strategy Head added a boost to the team's morale.

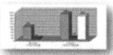

The statistics collated through the event tell their own success story. Special thanks to : John, Robert & Sylvia– for their significant contributions to design of the treasure Hunt Mugesan & Joe for creating and hosting the application on Intralink, Jack for helping with the mailers and Christeen for helping us with the visuals and processes that need to be followed

Some of the comments from the participants of this unique journey are -

- "It was a great experince in cracking the treasure hunt quiz set up to demonstrate how useful this information repository is to the people who wish to evolve technically. Getting acquainted with this data center has definitely enhanced my information lookup skills."

- "This was a very novel way of socializing the new technology. I really enjoyed completing the Treasure Hunt"

Figure 6-15. *Sample conclusion note to acknowledge the outcomes*

Benefit Assessment

After closure of the activity, it's recommended to conduct a measurement of the results. The adoption rate could be monitored later by survey to establish the continued realization of benefits from the investment in the Treasure Hunt. The survey could also be replaced with tracking statistics on the reduction in queries to the IT team or a reduced number of tickets opened with the technology support team.

CHAPTER 7

■ ■ ■

R2R Workshop

Context: Understanding Impact of Communication on Service Delivery

As the virtual office becomes reality, the ability to accurately understand stated and unstated expectations is a challenge. In many situations, the composition of stakeholders is varied and spread across different countries, speaking multiple languages in their unique accents. Hence, more than ever before, it is essential that messages be accurately communicated and understood. Communication also influences motivation levels of the employees, as unclear interactions lead to delays and forced repetition, creating confusion and frustration. New ideas and improvements are reduced or lost in miscommunication.

The phenomenon exemplified by the game of "Telephone" or "Whispers Down the Lane" is relevant to issues of misinterpretation and filling gaps in understanding with incorrect extrapolation. Errors in comprehension cause many problems like delay, loss of money, and falls in productivity due to rework, as well as avoidable complaints about services or products. For instance, a cryptic e-mail message could trigger a whole lot of escalation without any basis, causing disruption to the work, and on the other hand a well-structured document having details about expectations from the client can greatly benefit the flow of work.

Let's elaborate on various types of problems in communication. A team member, call her Jane in this example, is interacting with a client to understand the client's specific expectations, and then explaining these requirements to Bill, another team member, in a phone call or by e-mail. Jane may assume Bill will interpret the client's message exactly the way that Jane understood it. On the other hand, Bill has his own set of assumptions about and interpretations of the subject. The mental state of the person explaining and that of the listener or reader cannot be the same.

Differences in assumption and interpretation cause incomplete communication. The situation is compounded when the communication is in a medium that is not so familiar to either the person explaining or the person listening or reading. The medium here refers to new channels of communication, for example, messages sent over WhatsApp or Skype. These new channels of communication have crossed over from an informal medium to a formal one.

The difference in perspectives on how people interpret the message, particularly on a complex issue, leads to challenges in communication.

© Shreekant W Shiralkar 2016
S. W. Shiralkar, *IT Through Experiential Learning*, DOI 10.1007/978-1-4842-2421-2_7

Choosing a channel of communication that is not appropriate, such as e-mail or voicemail instead of a detailed document accompanied by an in-depth conversation, could complicate the situation further.

Poorly organized or written documents, including typos and mistakes, can also lead to misconceptions. Failing to give contextual information or inadequate detail is most often the biggest mistake. Unless both the team member explaining and the team member receiving the communication, either listening or reading, confirm that interpretation has been valid and all doubts have been clarified, the communication remains a single point of potential failure.

The aforesaid situation is the premise of the workshop explained in this chapter. The workshop includes a fun element while allowing participants to experience the criticality of communication to the software service delivery; it also helps participants realize that a problem, when understood, is more likely to be resolved than one that is left to assumption.

Most service delivery organizations are keen to improve productivity and reduced defect levels, especially those arising from communication. A workshop on communication and its impact on global team in a software service delivery organization was conceived. The workshop was titled "Requirement to Realization Workshop," a.k.a. "R2R Workshop." The workshop was designed to enable experiencing root causes of lower productivity and/or defects in service delivery. The workshop is intended to help participants learn to excel in translating client requirements and creating a positive experience in the process.

R2R Workshop is premised on creating a simulation of a real-world situation in a game-based approach; it's a game played by two teams, competing against each other, where they compete to draw a "visual" on the basis of narration by a "client." Both teams have to organize themselves into two sets of players. One set of players, the "onsite" members, listens to the narration of the visual and understanding it, and the rest, play counterparts as the "offshore" team or the team that is to draw the visual on a whiteboard. A person narrating the visual represents a client and describes a visual to onsite members from both teams when their offshore team members are not present. The onsite team in turn explains the visual to their offshore counterparts. The offshore team then draws the visual on the basis of their interpretation and understanding within the constraint of time. Both teams' drawings of the visual are compared with the original.

The team with the fewest deviations and with the fewest iterations is declared the winner. The scoring on the basis of deviations and iterations measures the difference between winner and loser. In the second round, workshop participants who were observers during the first round are invited to play the game; this time, another visual is used.

The game concludes with consolidation of individual and collective learning. The workshop requires a high level of participation and interactivity. The competitive aspect triggers intensity and depth of the experience, the element of gaming aids in maintaining a high interest level without stress, and the near-real-world simulation, facilitates comprehension of the subject (e.g., how eliminating assumptions raises the level of accuracy in realizing the requirement).

Figure 7-1 will help you visualize the workshop process.

The person representing the client holds the visual in his hand as he describes it to the onsite team members of both teams while their offshore colleagues are outside the hall.

Figure 7-1. Client narrates the visual to the onsite team members

The onsite team then explains the visual to their offshore counterparts. The offshore team then draws the visual on the whiteboard in the hall (Figure 7-2). The time taken is measured.

Figure 7-2. Offshore team members draw the visual on whiteboard

71

Both offshore teams draw the visuals on whiteboards in separate rooms on the basis of their understanding on visual from their onsite members (Figure 7-3).

Figure 7-3. *Realizing requirement on basis of information and interpretetion*

The deviations between the original and the whiteboard are listed for each team. The iterations between the onsite team and the offshore team and with the client are then counted. Finally, the score is tabulated on the basis of deviations and iterations.

An overview of the entire game is shown in Figure 7-4.

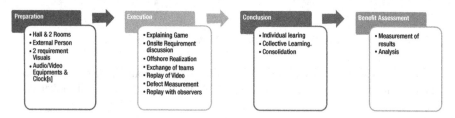

Figure 7-4. *R2R Workshop*

Activity

Let's now review the details of the activities in the process flow.

Preparation

1. Two visuals representing client requirements. (Picking visuals from an actual requirement document from the existing client repository is recommended.) Each of the visuals should have multiple types of charts and a variety of colors and fonts. The document should be complex enough to necessitate explanation and expression in oral form.

2. A well-defined set of rules is an essential prerequisite. It will help avoid grievances or conflicts among participants and most important it would avoid any possibility of loss of interest in the participants. It is recommended having a set of FAQ to respond to questions like "How many iterations can teams make?" or "What to do in case of doubt?"

3. Invite a person to represent a client.

It is recommended that a person who is a stranger to both teams and has not had any interaction prior to the workshop with any of the participants, will most accurately represent a client.

---

4. The venue of the workshop consists of the following:

   a. A large hall with an audiovisual recording and replay system. The hall should have a whiteboard.

   b. Two rooms adjacent to the hall. Each of the adjacent rooms should have a whiteboard for the offshore team's work and a large clock for display of time elapsed.

   c. Each room should be connected by a video conference unit and a telephone.

5. A set of rules and FAQ sheet that are published and clearly understood by all the participants.

6. A scoring sheet to measure deviations/defects.

Once all the preparation is complete, the game can begin.

Execution

The workshop begins with description of the context and the business implications to all the participants.

1. Volunteers from the participants are invited to form two teams of five each.

2. Among the team of five, two persons are identified as onsite and the other three as offshore.

3. The rest of the participants are observers and are requested to record each and every minute observation.

4. An external person is invited to play the role of client. He or she is then handed over one visual and given 5 minutes to understand and develop a narrative about it. The visual is then collected back by the instructor.

5. The team members from either team representing the offshore team are moved to the separate rooms adjacent to the hall.

6. Three volunteers from the rest of the participants are invited to play as monitors and timekeepers. Two of them move along with the offshore teams to their respective adjacent rooms.

7. The monitor in the hall announces the start of the time, and the person playing the role of client narrates the visual.

8. The onsite members get 5 minutes each to engage with the client and clarify their doubts; this is in addition to the collective discussion.

9. The onsite team gets 15 minutes to discuss and prepare themselves for relaying their understanding to their offshore team members.

10. One of the onsite team members from each of the teams is then sent to the room that holds their offshore team counterparts to interact and explain the visual to them. The time for explanation is limited to 5 minutes by the monitor in the room.

11. Each offshore team starts drawing the visual on the whiteboard in their room. They draw on the basis of their understanding and the input from their onsite members. They get 15 minutes to complete the drawing.

12. Five minutes after they start their attempt to replicate the visual, the offshore team members can seek clarification with their onsite members. However, each such clarification is counted as an iteration and is recorded by the monitor for the team, and is limited to 5 minutes each.

13. Once the offshore team declares completion or they have exhausted the time limit, the monitor of the room captures the visual and brings it to the hall for comparison with the original.

14. All gather in the hall for comparison and measurement of deviations from the original visual. Any deviation that has originated due to client's own interpretation or mistake is not counted as a deviation, since teams can draw the visual only on the basis of the client's interpretation.

15. The client shares feedback on the output, pointing out differences from his expectations.

16. Each team member is then requested to record his/her learning on how and why the differences representing work defects crept in without discussing it with any of the other participants.

17. The video recording of the entire workshop is replayed for participants to help observe and consolidate learning.

18. The game is then replayed by the observers (now the second round) in the same sequence. The person posing as the client uses the second visual.

19. Each of the team members now observing the activity are requested to identify the improvements or potential improvements in their notebook.

20. The replay of the process helps identify immediate improvements over the earlier process for translating the requirement to reality or recreating the visual with fewer deviations. The replay helps observers learn from their observations of the errors committed by others and therefore helps compound the impact of the learning on the participants.

21. Once the game is over, observations from experience are collected and crystallized in learning in the concluding section.

Conclusion

1. Each participant shares his/her learning. The learning is collated on a whiteboard and recorded as collective learning.

2. Each participant creates a plan to track and measure progress, based on learning for self-improvement.

3. An observer is given the collective learning sheet by the entire team as a reference to monitor progress in the future (Figure 7-5).

Figure 7-5. Instructor consolidating collective learning

Outcomes Based on Previous Workshops

1. A rapid-paced learning that otherwise needs a life cycle of project duration.

2. Learning many aspects of the requirement-gathering process and how to reach the final goal. Learning how to gather requirements that are never explained or articulated in conventional management practices.

Actual list of learning from one such workshop:

1. Communication plays vital role

2. Structured process that helps control assumptions and imaginations is more likely to generate better result. For example, devising a standard and comprehensive mode of communication with cross-validation feedback, simple language, and sequence of coverage on the subject from core to context.

3. Avoiding assumptions wherever possible is helpful. It is important to document assumptions very clearly and discuss every assumption with each stakeholder.

4. Ability to listen is, as essential, as clear and complete articulation/explanation.

5. Preparation for the client and his or her likely requirements, along with clarifications, that would help in ensuring complete documentation about the requirement, are necessary before getting into requirement gathering.

6. Focus on WHY rather than just WHAT?

Sample Artifacts

With a view to facilitate immediate application of the approach in the chapter, the following artifacts are provided in Figures 7-6 to 7-9:

1. A sample invitation message is shown in Figure 7-6.

2. A sample scoring sheet is shown in Figure 7-7.

3. Two sample visuals having reporting dashboards are shown in Figures 7-8 and 7-9.

SAMPLE INVITE LETTER

Dear <**NAME**>,

You are invited for a workshop on "Requirement to Realization" at <**VENUE**> on <**DATE**> @ <**TIME**>.

Workshop Brief :
The workshop will enable you learn and excel in delivering client requirements without error.

The workshop will be participative and is based on experiential mode of learning.

The workshop will be facilitated by <**INSTRUCTOR** > and <**EXTERNAL PERSON REPRESENTING CLIENT**> . .

About <**EXTERNAL PERSON REPRESENTING CLIENT**> : CIO at <**ORGANIZATION**>, A Senior IT Executive with with 20+ years of experience in deploying IT solutions Enterprise Solutions. Has led multiple transformation programs from planning to execution.

Pl block your calendar now and join us on coming <**DAY**> for a Learning experience workshop!

Looking forward to meeting you at the workshop,

Warm Regards
<**RSVP**>
Note : Workshop is limited to 15 participants. Please block your seat by sending an email to <**COORDINATOR**>

Figure 7-6. Sample invite message to participants

	No. of deviations	No. of iterations	Excess Time [in minutes]	Score
Overall Team				
Team - A				
Team - B				

Figure 7-7. Sample scoring sheet

Score calculation: Total Score = 100 – [no. of deviations + no. of deviations multiplied by no. of iterations] – [Time over budget in minutes]

Basis for scoring: Every deviation is a fault and loss of productivity. While iteration brings down the number of defects and deviation, it has a consequence on cost of quality. Therefore, any iteration reduces the overall score. Similarly, loss of time is deducted from the score.

The penalty for faults, the penalty for number of iterations, and the penalty for loss of time are factored...

The following are three different scenarios for calculation of score:

- Scenario 1: 12 deviations, 0 iterations, 5 minutes = 100 – [12+12×0]-[5] = 83

- Scenario 2: 5 deviations, 3 iterations, 0 minutes = 100 - [5+5×3] – [0] = 80

- Scenario 3: 8 deviations, 1 iteration, 10 minutes = 100 – [8+8×1] – [10] = 74

It is recommended that the scoring methodology is explained to the participants as part of the rules and published along with the FAQ.

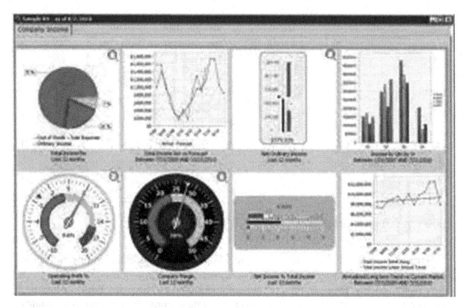

Figure 7-8. Sample visual #1

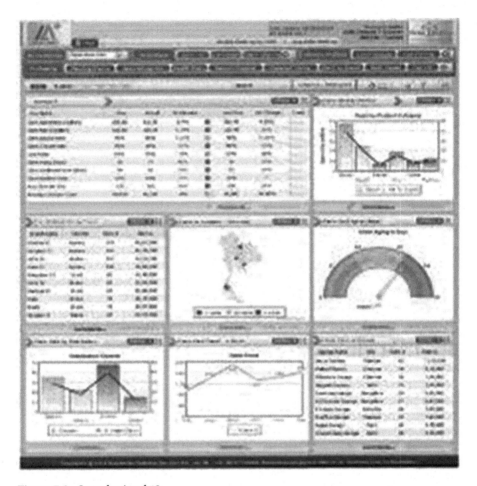

Figure 7-9. *Sample visual #2*

After consolidation of the learning, it's recommended to conduct a benefit assessment exercise to track and monitor the gains from application of the gamification.

Benefit Assessment

Each participant, as well as the team collectively, is kept on a self-assessment schedule for a month with target(s) based on the learning (e.g., number of defects resulting from communication, number of occurrences of deviation from actual requirements).

■ ■ ■

CHAPTER 8

Putting It All Together

We began the book by learning about the concept of experiential learning (EL) and its effectiveness over conventional methods in the first chapter. We then leveraged EL through the game-based approach to learn, adopt, deploy, and deliver, scenarios in IT. In this concluding chapter, I intend to motivate you, to apply your learning so far, and begin by expanding on the brief for four scenarios, then experiment by making changes to the games; finally, you graduate to experiencing the learning gained by designing new games for scenarios.

Expand

In this section, you will begin to experience, the learning gained so far, by expanding four new scenarios. Unlike the previous six chapters, games for the scenarios in this section are explained in brief and you would have to design rest of the details; you may refer to the templates and processes explained in earlier chapters for expanding on the brief. Here's the list of four scenarios that will need expanding and developing:

- Scenario 1. Understanding impact of perception

- Scenario 2. Collaborative reading: Developing collective interpretation on abstract concept

- Scenario 3. Teamwork: Understanding elements for better coordination

- Scenario 4. Impact of visibility and transparency

You will apply the learning to expand on the brief about the four scenarios in this chapter, and develop various aspects, especially the following:

- Preparation and planning

- Rules for playing the game

- Process flow

- Steps and sequence for execution of the game

- Mode of concluding or conducting the debrief session, including the benefit assessment

© Shreekant W Shiralkar 2016
S. W. Shiralkar, *IT Through Experiential Learning*, DOI 10.1007/978-1-4842-2421-2_8

Scenario 1: Understanding Impact of Perception

The game is played in two parts: the first part establishes what perception is and the second part allows experiencing the impact of perception. The game was conceived for a group of senior IT service delivery professionals who were unable to sense the impact of new technology and its likely impact on their future. To enable these service professionals to challenge their perception about the ecosystem and its stability, I conceived this game to enable experiencing the impact of perception.

The game consisted of two parts: in the first part, I used a transparent sheet to establish what perception is, and in the second part, the game allowed experiencing the impact of perception.

I initiated the group into the game by sharing a quote from Wayne Dyer: "*When you change the way you look at the things, the things you look at change*." Then, I showed a blank transparent sheet and inquired whether all agree that we are able to see same blank sheet. I then wrote the number "8" on the transparent sheet and again checked for consensus about the sheet's content; then, I added the number "1" to make number on the sheet become "18"; that's the time the audience disagreed with the number that I was seeing, as from the other side of the transparent sheet they were reading it, as number "81."

I engaged the group to discuss similar situations in life: how two persons looking in the same situation can reach different conclusions. I then established the context of how innovations in technology are causing disruption in the ecosystem, including the service delivery business, and unless the group challenges their perception of the status quo and is sensitive to the changes, as well as proactively leveraging the changes to stay ahead of the competition, they are likely to lose relevance. Then, two volunteers were invited to compete to deliver a service. Initially, both of them were sent out of the room, and then one was invited back in. I explained that the game was to be played by "filling water into a glass on table," which represents service delivery, and then I blindfolded him, contextualizing this as the perceptions and beliefs he carries while conducting the task. The time taken to complete the task was recorded, and the second volunteer was invited into the room. He too had the same task explained to him; however, in the second case, after blindfolding him, the water bottle on the table was discreetly replaced with an open-mouth jug. Due to the change of the container, the second volunteer took more time to complete the task (i.e., deliver the same service). The replacement of the bottle with a jug was contextualized as innovations, for example SaaS, which are changing the service delivery landscape rapidly and therefore require service professionals to challenge their perceptions and beliefs and be sensitive to change, to identify new and emerging opportunities for proactive engagement.

Figure 8-1 will help you visualize the game of perception.

The instructor stands in front of the audience holding a transparent sheet. Initially, nothing is written, but next, the instructor writes number 8 and shows it to the participants, and then he writes number 18, which the audience reads as 81.

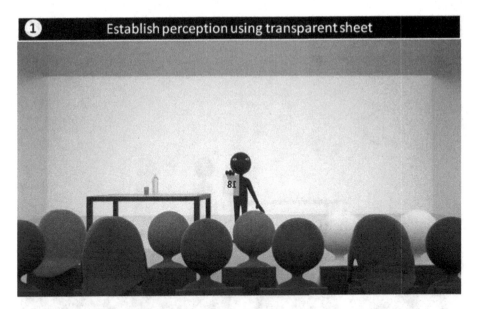

Figure 8-1. Instructor establishing perception

In second part of the game, a volunteer is invited to perform a task. The task is explained as simply filling water from bottle to glass placed next to it on the table. The glass needs to be filled approximately halfway.

The volunteer is then blindfolded. The instructor announces the start of the activity and helps the volunteer to reach the table. The time taken to complete the task is measured and recorded on the whiteboard in the hall (Figure 8-2).

Figure 8-2. Understanding the task for static environment

Another volunteer from the group is invited to perform the same task. The volunteer is then blindfolded. The instructor announces the start of the activity and helps the volunteer to reach the table. However, instructor discreetly, replaces the bottle on the table with a water jug. The volunteer usually fumbles before realizing that task can be performed with the jug as well and that the task was defined as filling the glass with water; there was no specific instruction about whether the water is to be sourced from a bottle or a jug. Most probably, the volunteer inquires about the possibility of whether water can be poured from the jug. The process, however, is at the expense of time. The time taken to complete the task is measured and recorded on the whiteboard in the hall (Figures 8-3 and 8-4).

Figure 8-3. *Performing task in static environment*

Figure 8-4. *Performing task in changed environment*

Scenario 2: Collaborative Reading—Developing Collective Interpretation of Abstract Concept

In this situation, I was assigned role with key responsibility for growth of thought leadership with IT professionals from a technology practice. In my observation, most professionals in the practice understood and appreciated the basic concept of thought leadership. However, understanding of the relevance and impact of thought leadership for each individual and also collectively to the whole group was not consistent, and there was wide variation in comprehension.

With a view to create a collective and relevant understanding of the subject, I conceived a group activity of collective reading. The activity included having debate before arriving at a consensus-based understanding of the subject. I used the overhead projector to present a definition of thought leadership on a screen in the hall. I had ensured that the screen was visible to everyone in the hall. I also introduced following rules:

1. A participant should raise his or her hand before speaking and avoid talking when another participant is speaking.

2. Each word is read out and its meaning and positioning in the statement are explained.

3. Multiple perspectives/interpretations are essential.

4. Debate is essential for appreciating all the different views and interpretations before arriving at the consensus.

Figure 8-5 will help you visualize the process.

Figure 8-5. *Collective reading to establish "unified interpretation"*

The instructor projects the text on the subject. The audience can be divided into two sides. They are then invited to start reading the text word by word and share interpretations and understandings of the text. Each key word in the text is thoroughly discussed and debated, and a collective understanding is developed. Use of a whiteboard can aid making notes on some of the aspects to be referred to, in the concluding part for consolidation of the learning.

Scenario 3: Teamwork—Understanding Elements for Better Coordination

In the third situation, I was tasked with the responsibility to enhance team coordination. I designed a game that was premised on my learning from a game in the childhood.

During my childhood, my friends and I enjoyed the game of tag with blindfold, where one of us was blindfolded and had to catch each one of the others to finish his turn before passing over to the person who was the first caught. The game was played in a clearly defined space which put constraints on the people who had to dodge while being chased by the blindfolded person. In the game some of us could finish our turn for being blindfolded faster as a catcher than others. In my observations, I noted that those friends who had better ability to judge space and visualize surroundings and who were better listeners finished their blindfold turn earlier than others, and over the years were more sought after in the team games because of their ability to coordinate easily with others.

In my assignment, I engaged a group of leaders attending a leadership program at the management development institute on the subject of effective communication and attempted to help them assess their own abilities or limitations; I designed a blindfold game premised on the game described earlier. The game helped in beating the limitations of the blindfolded person by allowing oral instructions from the partner. The partner had to communicate effectively to ensure that the blindfolded team member finishes the task faster and better. The results of the game overwhelmed the participants as it brought forward the criticality of effective communication and elements of coordination in teamwork.

Aforesaid is the premise of the activity that will be explained in this section. The activity induces a direct assessment on effective communication and team coordination and its impact on the speed and quality of the outcome.

The game is to draw a star within the constraint of outer and inner boundaries (Figure 8-6). The red rectangle represents the outside boundary and the red circle inside represents the inner boundary. The blindfolded participant has to draw a star with a green whiteboard marker pen. The star is drawn with help and instructions of partner, who will verbally instruct the blindfolded participant. The red boundaries can't be touched by the star.

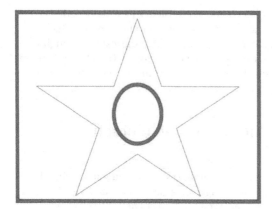

Figure 8-6. Draw star within two red boundaries

Both the boundaries are drawn along with a reference picture on the whiteboard in the hall. A person blindfolded with pen under instruction from his partner draws the star while competing on the basis of speed and quality with another team of two performing the same activity (Figure 8-7).

Figure 8-7. Teams of two compete to draw star

I had designed the following rules for the game:

1. The partner has to give instructions verbally only and cannot guide the blindfolded person through any physical contact.

2. In case the blindfolded person touches either the circle or rectangle, then the entire star will have to be redrawn (i.e., the activity has to start from the beginning); however, the time consumed up to the error will get added to the overall time taken to complete the task.

3. The distance between the instructing partner and the blindfolded person will be same for each of the competing teams.

Material:

1. Whiteboard

2. Whiteboard marker pens

3. Audiovisual recording equipment

Consolidating Learning:
The difference in the time needed by two teams provides the basic premise to start the analysis to identify learning elements from the experience.

a. Invite all participants/observers to read from their notepads and share three learnings each from the experience.

b. Use the second whiteboard to start recording the elements of learning.

■ **Variations** The star could be replaced with a simpler shape like a triangle. Instead of the outer rectangle a circle could represent the outer limit. People can be made to switch roles to assess difference as well as improvements in subsequent attempts.

Scenario 4: Impact of Visibility and Transparency

Information technology and solutions directly impact visibility and transparency in transactions and therefore aid efficiency. With a view to demonstrate the impact of transparency on efficiency, I engaged a group of MBA students to perform a simple task of filling a glass with water, with and without blindfolding, and show the difference of time taken. The blindfold represents systems lacking transparency, while the having open eyes during task performance represents the benefit of IT that provides a comprehensive view of parameters and environment (Figure 8-8).

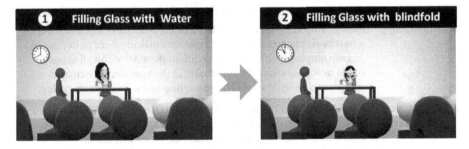

Figure 8-8. Activity to establish impact of transparency

In applying the learning to detail the gamification for four scenarios in this chapter, you have experienced the ability to expand on the brief and apply the game-based approach for the scenarios. Now I invite you to move further and venture into experimenting by modifying elements of the game to apply for different contexts or improving effectiveness.

Experiment

Initially, you could apply your learning to enhance the games in terms of the details of each element in the scenario; once you experience and understand the process, you would be able to conceive and create completely new games.

Each of the games so far has been explained in the context of a specific situation; for example, the bidding game for developing a collective understanding of the subject of ERP, or Treasure Hunt for individual learning on features and facilities within a newly implemented software solution.

In the following section, I will now introduce application of the same games to different situations and extend coverage of previously used cases, while providing clues for your experiments, with the game-based approach.

Modify Games for New Situations/Contexts

Each case provided so far gave you a ready-to-use gamification approach. Now I invite you to use a little imagination and creativity to extend the application of these games to other situations. To help you experiment and respond to my invitation, Table 8-1 lists alternative situations.

Table 8-1. *Alternative Gamification Scenarios*

Game	Possible Situation/Context
Bidding Game	Could be used for growing collective awareness on new technology, for example "cloud computing." Develop a comprehensive list of questions to cover the basic relevant aspects of cloud computing.
Treasure Hunt	Could be used for facilitating accelerated awareness and adoption of a new business process, for example new procurement policy; would engage employees to read and acquaint themselves on all aspects of the new policy starting from basic to the specific. Participants progress from level to level by answering questions on new policy.
Blindfold Game	Could be used to identify level of essential leadership skill, for example communication and delegation within a set of participants; would help establish the level of skill and therefore enable prioritizing person-specific training needs.

After you've experimented and experienced your ability to use the games for newer situations and contexts, you are invited, in the following section, to go further and experience the game-based approach to newer situations and contexts.

Experience

Earlier, I invited you to apply your learning to develop the games detailed for different situations and benefit from the effectiveness of the game-based approach. I now invite you to experience your ability to apply learning from the book and modify gaming elements of the current games or even create completely new games to apply EL using the game-based approach and develop solutions to your IT situations.

I recommend the following considerations listed here and provided in Figure 8-9 while designing games:

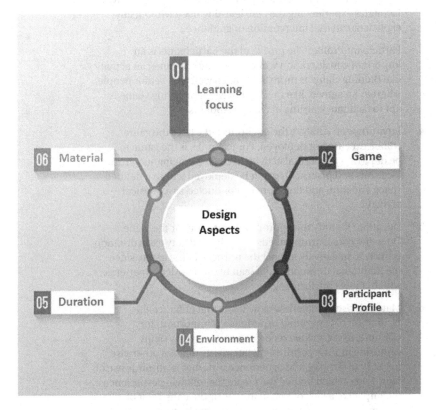

Figure 8-9. *Considerations for game design*

1. Learning Focus: Identify core learning need from the game. Learning is premised on observations which are drawn from the experience. So, for a learning need, identify the experience that can facilitate observation, leading to the target learning. Here's an example of the process: to learn the impact of perception on efficiency, create a game that facilitates experiencing perception and ensure that the participants are able to observe the impact. The impact on efficiency could be physically measured and evidenced.

2. Game: Ensure that the process of learning is self-governed through experience, and facilitation is managed through context setting for the game. Map the experience of the core learning need for a game or activity; for example, to experience individual behavior change, the individual can be asked to discuss individually as well as present the same idea to a crowd; this could also be to enact the idea to add an element of fun. Adding competition in constraint of time always ensures that intensity to experience the core need by the participant is heightened. The most critical part is to ensure that the activity facilitates experiencing the core learning need without any explicit or external intervention or guidance.

3. Participant Profile: The profile of the participants is an important consideration while designing the game; an activity like Bidding Game is more likely to go well with senior people, whereas an activity like the Aircraft Manufacturing Game is apt to facilitate learning of college students.

4. Environment: Analyze the environment where the game will be executed or deployed. For example, is the game to be deployed as a virtual activity to cover participants across locations and places? Or can it be deployed within a defined space and time and therefore be conducted as a physical activity?

5. Duration: Identify the appropriate duration for the game. Once the core learning needs are delivered, any extra duration is likely to negatively impact the purpose of the game, since the additional duration could lead to unintended experience which dilutes the learning.

6. Material: Use of materials or artifacts that enhance the facilitation of generating experience is important; for example, using a video recording and its replay helps capturing minute gestures or statements that are otherwise not easy to observe and experience. Another example is use of blindfolds, which helped me create the following experiences: the impact of a lack of transparency, or the constraint of a team member not having the entire "Big Picture" of the program, or just plain and simple "bias".

Table 8-2 provides clues for innovating and modifying the current games.

Table 8-2. *Modifying Your Games*

Game	Modification	Situation
Ship Manufacturing Game	The game could replace an aircraft with a ship	
Blindfold Game	After consolidation of learning for the group, throw a challenge for two people from the nonplayers to beat the best time and replay the game with variation that the table/chairs/jug/glass would be kept in a completely different arrangement; for example, chairs in the middle and table with its legs facing upward.	The modification would consolidate the learning as well as make the additional point that learning by experience is far superior to observation.

(continued)

Table 8-2. (*continued*)

Game	Modification	Situation
R2R Workshop	In a team of three, one person gets to see the requirement (i.e., the sheet of paper) for about 1 minute and then he/she describes it to a second team member, who in turn explains to the last team member, who has to draw his/her understanding on a whiteboard in a specified amount of time.	Critical importance of comprehension and importance of observation/listening in communication.

In your quest to create new games and engage in gamification for IT, I would suggest referring to the following videos on YouTube to get new ideas for game design:

- `https://youtu.be/CpgGqwf0h48` (for group cohesion)

- `https://youtu.be/gcy-pkwLjXE` (for effective communication)

Summary

The content of the book first introduced you to the concepts of EL and the game-based approach and then gradually exposed you to the application of the approach for different situations and contexts in IT.

In this concluding chapter you were motivated to build on the learning in earlier chapters by expanding and developing on the brief for four scenarios, which enabled you to identify gaming elements that could be experimented with to raise effectiveness levels or to apply them to changed contexts. At the conclusion, you were invited to experience the knowledge gained from the book by creating games for newer scenarios and exploit the effectiveness of EL and the high level of engagement of participants when the game-based approach is taken.

Index

Get the eBook for only $4.99!

Why limit yourself?

Now you can take the weightless companion with you wherever you go and access your content on your PC, phone, tablet, or reader.

Since you've purchased this print book, we are happy to offer you the eBook for just $4.99.

Convenient and fully searchable, the PDF version enables you to easily find and copy code—or perform examples by quickly toggling between instructions and applications.

To learn more, go to http://www.apress.com/us/shop/companion or contact support@apress.com.